1 MONTH OF
FREE
READING

at

www.ForgottenBooks.com

By purchasing this book you are eligible for one month membership to ForgottenBooks.com, giving you unlimited access to our entire collection of over 1,000,000 titles via our web site and mobile apps.

To claim your free month visit:

www.forgottenbooks.com/free103721

ISBN 978-0-484-28517-9
PIBN 10103721

AN

ADDRESS,

DELIVERED AT THE

CENTENNIAL CELEBRATION,

IN

PETERBOROUGH, N.H.

OCT. 24, 1839.

BY JOHN HOPKINS MORISON.

BOSTON,

PRINTED BY ISAAC R. BUTTS,

A HUNDRED years ago this whole valley, from mountain to mountain, from the extreme north to the extreme southern limit, was one unbroken forest. The light soil upon the banks of the Contoocook was covered with huge and lofty pines, while the rocky hills and rich loamy lands were shaded with maple, beech and birch, interspersed with ash, elm, hemlock, fir, oak, cherry, bass, and other kinds of wood. Bogs and swamps were far more extensive then than now ; and the woods in many parts, on account of the fallen timber and thick underbrush, were almost impassable. The deer and the moose roamed at large ; the wolf and bear prowled about the hills ; the turkey and partridge whirred with heavy flight from tree to tree, while the duck swam undisturbed upon the lonely, silent waters. The beaver and the freshet made the only dam that impeded the streams in their whole course from the highlands to the Merrimack ; the trout, pickerel and salmon moved through them unmolested, while the old Monadnoc, looking down in every direction upon almost interminable forests, saw in the hazy distance the first feeble encroachments upon the dominion which he had retained over his wild subjects for more than a thousand years.

That an attempt was made to settle this town as early as 1739 there can be no doubt. The authority of the petition for incorporation as a town, of which, through the Secretary of State, we have been favored with a copy, is on this point decisive. The town was surveyed and laid out by Joseph Hale, Jr. in 1737. Of the party that came in 1739 no memorial remains. Probably they were driven away before any considerable clearing had been made. In 1742 five men,* each with an axe and a small supply of provisions upon his shoulders, came from Lunenburg, Mass., and cleared a few small patches of land near the old Meeting-house. They abandoned the settlement at, or more probably considerably before, the alarm of war in 1744. Soon after this party three men cut down the brush and girdled the large trees on the hill near the Ritchie-place at the south part of the town, but left before they had put in their seed. They probably returned the next year with Thomas Morison and John Swan. It could not have been later than 1744, and must have been at a period when there were no other settlers here. For it is a story often told by the children of Thomas Morison, and which cannot well be doubted, that soon after they came, several Indians called upon them just after breakfast, appeared friendly, and, after tarrying a short time, went away. When the cook, however, came from chopping to prepare a dinner for the party, he found not only the pot which he had left upon the fire robbed of its contents, but all their provisions carried off; and they were obliged to go to Townsend, twenty-five miles, for a dinner; which they would not have done had there been other inhabitants here at the time.

In 1744 the town was entirely abandoned, and the settlement was not resumed till the peace of 1749. Indeed, I have

* The traditions are by no means distinct, and it is possible that this party came as early as 1739. They may not have staid more than a single season. Their names, according to Mr. Dunbar, (see N. H. Historical Collections, Vol. I, p. 129) were William Robbe, Alexander Scott, Hugh Gregg, William Gregg and Samuel Stinson. John Todd, senior, a high authority in the antiquities of our town, says they were William Scott, William Robbe, William Wallace, William Mitchell and Samuel Stinson.

The second party were William M'Nee, John Taggart, William Ritchie.

found little evidence that families* had established themselves here previous to that period, and this presumption is confirmed by the fact that the first male child, John Ritchie, was not born till February 22, 1751. All that was done therefore previous to the war of '44 was only to prepare the way for the future settlement, which was commenced in earnest in 1749. From that time the colony was rapidly increased by new accessions from abroad till in '59 there were forty-five or fifty families, from Lunenburg, Londonderry, and some immediately from Ireland. They all, however, belonged to the same stock. They came to this country from the north of Ireland, and were usually called Scotch-Irish.

Early in the reign of James I, † on the suppression of a rebellion by his Catholic subjects in the north of Ireland, two millions of acres of land, almost the whole of the six northern counties, including Londonderry, fell to the king; and his Scotch and English subjects were encouraged by liberal grants to leave their own country, and settle on these lands, in order to keep in awe the turbulent spirits, who had so often defied the authority and arms of the British government. This accounts in some measure for the hatred which the English and Scotch population bore to the Catholics, who could not but hate the men who occupied the soil from which their countrymen had been forcibly expelled. The great Irish rebellion — for they were many — which happened thirty years after, in the reign of his son, doubtless had its origin in the attempt of the Irish Catholics to extort the redress of grievances and repel religious persecution; and we may well suppose that they had not yet forgotten the transfer of their property to foreigners of a religion different from their own. The plot of a general massacre of the Protestants was discovered in the southern part of the kingdom before the time fixed for its execution; but this was unknown in Ulster, and the most cruel destruction of lives

---

* Catharine Gregg, mother of Gov. Miller, is said to have been baptised here in 1743.

* Lingard, Vol. IX, 121. Hume, Vol. VI, 433 — 6.

and property ensued that has ever stained the bloody pages of history. Some of the first settlers of our Derry were probably alive at the time.

John Morison,* my great, great, grandfather, who died here in 1776, was born about thirty years after, but you may well suppose that vivid pictures of this dreadful time, when, according to some,† not less than one hundred and fifty thousand were victims, had been strongly impressed upon his mind.

In order better to understand these people from whom we are descended, we must remember, that in addition to those already mentioned, in the time of Cromwell, about 1656,‡ a large number of English and Scotch, mostly Scotch, were induced to settle in Ireland on lands forfeited for the Popish rebellion of 1641, or by the adherents of the king. All these circumstances must have greatly exasperated the original Catholic Irish against the foreigners who had thus been planted among them.

In 1689, James II. returned from France. His intention was to settle the affairs of Ireland. On the first alarm of an intended massacre the Protestants flew to arms and shut themselves up in the strong places, particularly in Londonderry, where, under the command of Walker, an Episcopal clergyman, they defended themselves against the royal army. The ships sent to them with supplies were kept back by a boom across the entrance of the harbor, below the city. The French general who commanded the besiegers, threatened to raze the city to its foundations and destroy every man, woman and child, unless they would immediately submit to James. But these brave men, suffering at the time from hunger and every privation, treated the Popish general's threats with contempt. His next step was to drive the inhabitants, for thirty miles round, under the walls of the city. Among these miserable beings,

* I have retained the spelling for this name which was used by his sons Thomas and Jonathan in their signature to the petition for incorporation in 1759. It is the true Scotch orthography.

† Hume, Vol. VI, 436 — 7.

‡ Hume, Vol. VII, 268.

exceeding four thousand in number, was the family of John Morison, then nine years old. The greater part, after being detained there three days without tasting food, were suffered to return to their habitations, plundered of every thing, and many of them actually dying upon the road of hunger and fatigue. His family were admitted into the famished city. The garrison, which consisted of about seven thousand, became greatly reduced * in numbers ; but their courage and constancy remained unshaken. Just when their sufferings had reached the point beyond which human nature can suffer no more, Gen. Kirk, who had deserted his master and joined King William, sent two ships laden with provisions and convoyed by a frigate, to sail up the river. One of them, after two unsuccessful attempts, and amidst a hot fire from both sides of the channel, at length reached the wharf to the inexpressible joy of the inhabitants.

There are now alive† those who have frequently heard this youth, when near a hundred years old, relate the most striking incidents of the siege.—Standing upon the walls of the city, where he could survey at once the besieging army surrounding them, and full of a more savage cruelty than any other army had ever possessed ; ready to execute their threats of indiscriminate rage and slaughter against the miserable sufferers within,— the frigate and transports just heaving in sight, the foremost in full sail, with a strong wind, prepared to cut the boom. Amid a severe fire from the enemy, on both sides of the channel, she strikes against it and bounds heavily back, to the consternation of the inhabitants. Again she advances, new hopes are kindled ; she strikes and again bounds heavily back in full sight of the pale and starving multitude. A third attempt is made ; the chain creaks and breaks. The old man could resume the

---

* Burnet says that near two-thirds of them perished by hunger.—Burnet's Own Time, Vol. III, p. 20.

† This whole account I have received from his grandson, Hon. Jeremiah Smith, who remembers distinctly the tall, erect form, the engaging countenance, urbane manners, and " peculiar native eloquence," which, together with the remarkable scenes through which he had passed, made a strong impression upon the young.

boy and describe most graphically the universal joy, when the ships reached the city.

I have dwelt long on this part of the subject.—For John Morison, the oldest man that was ever buried in our place, had among our early settlers, three sons, four sons-in-law, and the numerous family of Steeles * were descended from his sister; so that he has been connected far more extensively than any other man with our inhabitants, and may in some measure be looked back upon as the patriarch of the town. † But in addition to this, it is necessary to bear in mind the circumstances that have been mentioned, in order to understand the character of the emigrants from the north of Ireland. They have been often confounded with the Irish, and yet at the time of their emigration, there were perhaps no two classes in the United Kingdom more unlike, or more hostile. Every circumstance in their history, for more than a hundred years, had served only to inflame them against each other. The original strong traits, which separate the Scotch and Irish, had been gathering strength through more than a century of turbulence and bloodshed, in which they had been constantly exasperated against each other by their interests, by secret plots and open rebellions, by cruel massacres, by civil wars carried on through the most black and malignant of all passions, religious hatred.

It is not, therefore, wonderful that even after the establishment of the Protestant cause by the accession of William, Anne and the house of Hanover to the throne of Great Britain, they should still have found their position in Ireland uncomfortable. They considered themselves a branch of the Scotch Presbyterian church, and though permitted to maintain their own forms of worship unmolested, a tenth part of all their increase was rigorously exacted for the support of the established Episcopal church.—

* Capt. Thomas Steele came in 1763 from Londonderry, N. H.

† By marriage, or direct descent, he has been connected with the families of Steele, Wilson, Smith, Wallace, Moore, Mitchell, Todd, Jewett, Gregg, Ames, Holmes, Gray, Field, Stuart, Little, Swan, and probably some others, without including the last generation.

They also held their lands and tenements by lease, and not as the proprietors of the soil.* They were a religious people with an inextinguishable thirst for liberty, and could not therefore bear to be trammeled in their civil and religious rights.

For these reasons, and influenced particularly by the representations of a young man named Holmes, the son of a clergyman, who had been here, four Presbyterian ministers, † with a large portion of their congregations, determined to remove to this country. They belonged not to the lowest class in the country from which they came, but perhaps to the lower portion of the middling class. They had the cool heads which their fathers had brought from Scotland, and doubtless counted well the cost of the step they were about to take. It required no small strength of character to leave a country where they *could* live quietly and in tolerable comfort, for an untried region, with an ocean between, and a full prospect before them of the labors and sufferings incident to planting a new country with slender means. In the summer of 1718, they embarked in five ships for America.‡ About one hundred families arrived in Boston § Aug. 4; and twenty families more in one of the vessels, landed at Casco-Bay, now Portland. Among these were three of the families (Gregg, Morison and Steele,) who afterwards settled in Peterborough. The vessel had intended to put in at Newburyport; but arrived at Casco-Bay so late in the season, that she

* See Century Sermon, by Rev. Edward L. Parker, of Londonderry, p. 7. See also Farmer's Belknap, p. 191.

† Holmes, James M'Gregore, William Cornwell and William Boyd. The Federal St. Church in Boston was founded by this same class of emigrants.

‡ From a manuscript left by Rev. James M'Gregore, and seen by Mr. Parker, it would appear that he preached to them on leaving Ireland, stating distinctly that they were coming to America in order " to avoid oppression and cruel bondage ; to shun persecution and designed ruin ; to withdraw from the communion of idolaters, and to have an opportunity of worshiping God according to the dictates of conscience and the rules of the inspired word."

§ They brought with them, according to Dr. Belknap, the first little wheels turned by the foot that were used in the country, and the first potatoes planted in New-England ; which from them have ever since been called *Irish* potatoes.

was frozen in, and they, unable to provide more comfortable quarters, were obliged to spend the whole winter on board, suffering severely from the want of suitable accommodations and food. It is said that on first landing upon that cold and cheerless coast, the wintry ocean behind them and naked forests before, after the solemn act of prayer, they united in singing that most touching of all songs: — " By the rivers of Babylon, there we sat down, yea, we wept, when we remembered Zion ; " and with peculiar feelings as they surveyed the waste around them, and remembered the pleasant homes which they had left, might they add, " How shall we sing the Lord's song in a strange land ? "

They left Casco-Bay early in the spring, and began their settlement in Londonderry, April 11th, O. S., 1719. The people of the neighboring towns, supposing them to be Irish, harbored strong prejudices against them, and wished to have them driven out from the country. Soon after they began their settlement in Londonderry, a party from Haverhill, headed by one Herriman, came in order forcibly to expel them. It was on Friday afternoon, and the settlers, with their wives and children, had come together under an old oak, to attend, according to the good old Presbyterian fashion, the lecture preparatory to the communion, which was to be administered the following Sabbath. Herriman stopped his party and listened till the services were over, when, deeply affected by what he had seen and heard, he said to his followers, " Let us return ; it is vain to attempt to disturb this people ; for surely the Lord is with them."*

In Sept. 1736 or '37, another party came over from Ireland. Among them. were the Smiths, the Wilsons and Littles. Mrs. Sarah M'Nee, or, as she was called, old Aunt Nay, who died within my memory, aged 97, (or, as some supposed, one hundred years old, was one of this party, and used to relate with much satisfaction, that as the vessel approached the wharf

* This account I have taken partly from Mr. Parker's Sermon, and partly from the lips of John Todd, sen.

in Boston, a gentleman there, after inspecting them closely, said, " Truly, these are no poor folk, and," she always added, " he was an awfu' great gentleman ; for he had ruffles on his fingers." It* was noised about that a pack of Irishmen had landed, and they were much annoyed by the observations that were made upon them. " Why," said one, with evident surprise, " these people are white.' " So they are," said another, with not less astonishment, " as white as you or I." " It made my blood boil," said the elder William Smith, who was then about eighteen years old, " to hear ourselves called a parcel of Irish." The prejudice subjected them to a more serious inconvenience, and rendered it difficult to procure lodgings. They however succeeded in getting a Mr. Winship, in the east part of Lexington, to take them for the winter. His neighbors, espe-cially during the intermission on Sundays, would crowd around him and remonstrate loudly against his harboring these Irishmen. At last he would listen no longer, but told them that if his house reached to Charlestown, and he could find such Irish as these, he would have it filled up with Irish, and none but Irish."

The spring or summer following (1737), they came to Lunenburg, Mass. from which place, and from Londonderry, small parties, as we have seen, came out between '39 and '49 to make a settlement in Peterborough. The township had been granted by the General Court of Massachusetts, on the suppo-sition that it was within their limits, to Samuel Haywood† and others, but soon after was transferred to the famous Jeremiah Gridley of Boston, John Hill, Fowle and William Vassal, who were become the sole proprietors of the soil. Under pur-chases made from them, the first settlements were made, and the town took its name from Peter Prescott, of Concord, Mass.

* For this I am indebted to my great aunt, Sally Morison, who, though always feeble, and for many years an invalid, retains now, in her 85th year, a very perfect recollection of what she heard more than seventy years ago.

† The petition for incorporation (Oct. 31, 1739) says, * * " in consequence of a tract of land had and obtained from the Great and General Court or As-sembly of the Province of the Massachusetts Bay, by Samuel Haywood and others, his associates," &c.

Till 1749, almost nothing was done. It is impossible to say how many came then; but from that time the growth was rapid. The hardships of the first settlers cannot be understood from anything that is now experienced by the pioneers in our western territories. Being recently from a foreign country, they were unaccustomed to the axe, and by no means acquainted with the best method of clearing away the timber, and yet, here they were in the midst of an unbroken forest, to which alone they must look for support. The gloom and loneliness of the place, the hollow echoing of the hills and woods as the first tall pine fell groaning by their side, the sound of strange birds and insects, the dismal creaking and howling among the trees upon a stormy night, connected with what they had heard of destructive beasts and snakes, and the frightful acts of Indian cruelty which were going on all around them, must have made an impression upon them which we can hardly conceive. Add to these, the superstitious fears, the religious awe that overcame them as they stood here, apart from the civilized abode of man, and it will not seem strange if again and again they abandoned what they had begun even from imaginary fears, and withdrew that they might for a season be within the sympathy and security of an older settlement. A single incident will show the constant apprehension under which they lived. About twelve o'clock, on one of those autumnal nights, when the moon rising late, hangs with a sort of supernatural gloom over the horizon, the family of William Smith were suddenly startled from their sleep by shrieks of murder in the house of their nearest neighbor. Immediately, without waiting to put on a single garment, the father and mother, each with a child, left their log-hut, and forcing their way, no one could ever tell how, more than two miles through the woods, arrived at the log-house of her brother, (near where the South Fac ory now is) and spread the alarm, that they had barely escaped with their lives from the Indians. Capt. Thomas Morison, who was a man of greater martial coolness than his brother-in-law, after supplying them with clothes, joined them with his own wife and children, one an infant, and after hiding them in the woods south of his house, set out for the fort, about a mile further south, saying as he left them, that if he should meet the enemy before reaching the fort they would know it, because he should certainly have time to fire, and kill at least one man before he should himself he killed or taken. Meanwhile, the Swans, another family at the south, had taken the alarm and fled for the fort. Soon after, a younger Swan returning home at that late hour, from what to young men is a very pleasant as well as important business, and finding his father's boots and clothes by the bedside, and the house deserted, ran out almost frantic and spread the report that his whole family had been murdered and carried away by the Indians. The consternation was general and intense ; and it was not discovered till morning that the whole panic was occasioned by some thoughtless young men at Mr. Cunningham's, who had screamed and shrieked simply to frighten their neighbors, the Smiths.

This incident, trifling as it is, shows the constant apprehension in which our fathers every night retired to their beds ; and yet they were brave men. About the same time with this alarm, perhaps the following summer, a report was spread here that the Indians had fallen upon the settlements at Keene. Immediately Capt. Morison with his company set out, and in the heat of summer, marched more than twenty miles through the woods to rescue their brethren from an enemy of unknown strength, who seldom spared a foe. Upon arriving at Keene, the men there were found mowing peaceably in the field, and so much were they affected by this act of kindness, that they could not re rain from weeping.*

Such was the continual fear of midnight fire and murder from the Indians for twenty years from the commencement of the settlement ; being several times, as their petition says, driven off by the enemy, and " many of them almost ruined." " Yet," to use their own affecting language, " what little we had in the

* This was told me by his daughter, Elizabeth Morison.

world lay there ; we having no whither else to go, returned to our settlement as soon as prudence would admit, where we have continued since, and cultivated a rough part of the wilderness to a fruitful field."

But aside from the apprehension of danger, they surely had difficulties and hardships enough. Till 1751, they had no grist-mill, and were obliged to bring all their provisions upon their shoulders five-and-twenty miles. For many years there was not a glass window in the place. Their dwellings were miserable huts, not a board upon or within them till 1751, when three frame houses were erected. Most of the frame houses first made, were poorly built. In one,* considerably later than this, when the family had gathered round the table, the floor suddenly gave way just as the good man was asking a blessing, and the whole party, dinner and all, found themselves in the cellar. The first meeting house,† which must have been erected as early as 1752 or 1753, for several years was furnished with no other seats than rough boards laid loosely upon square blocks of wood. For a long period there were no oxen, and still later no horses. The first mill-stone used, was drawn (in 1751) more than a mile and a half by seventeen men and boys. Their food was meagre in kind, and not often abundant in quantity. Bean porridge, potatoes and samp (corn) broth were for the first twenty years the principal articles of diet. The women vied with the men, and sometimes excelled them in the labors of the field. There was no bridge till 1755, and the roads were fit only for foot passengers. But notwithstanding their privations and hardships, with insufficient clothing and almost without shoes, except in the severest weather, the first settlers lived to

* The house was William Moore's, and William Smith, Esq. the man who was asking the blessing as they sunk.

† It was thirty feet square, and stood a little to the east of what we call the " old meeting-house," which was raised in 1777. During the raising, a deep gloom was thrown over the whole assembly by the arrival of a courier, who announced that our troops had left Ticonderoga, and that a new levy was called for. In 1760 the first meeting-house was enlarged by an addition in front, considerably broader than the main body.

an unusually advanced period, and the three oldest people that have ever died in the place were natives of Ireland, and among our earliest inhabitants.*

Such was the condition of the town for the first twenty years after its settlement. About that period many new comforts began to be introduced. Oxen became more common. The richer part of the inhabitants might be seen going to meeting on horseback, the good man before, his wife on the pillion behind; while at noon the children would gather round with almost envious eyes to admire this curious and sumptuous mode of conveyance. All marketing was done with a horse. Butter was carried by tying two casks together and placing them across the horse's back like panniers. In this way the wife of Major Wilson often carried her spare articles to Boston, while her son James was in Harvard College, between the years 1785 and '89. The first chaise was introduced in 1793, and the first one horse w gon in 1810.

Few things could have given our ancestors more annoyance than their extreme awkwardness in the mechanical arts.† For this reason their houses must have been loose, cold, and deficient in almost every article of domestic convenience. Jonathan Morison‡ was the first, and for a considerable time, the only mechanic in town. He was a mill-wright, a blacksmith, a carpenter, a house-joiner, a stone-cutter, a gun-maker, and had the reputation of being really a workman at all these trades. He was the son of John Morison, and was considered the most gifted of the family, being a man of quick parts, great ingenuity

* John Morison and Sarah M'Nee, who died in their 98th, and Mrs. Cunningham in her 99th year.

† This was well taken off by uncle Mosey (as every one called him) in his account of Deacon Duncan's hewing, and Deacon Moore's ladder. "As I was ganging," said he, "thro' the woods, I heard a desprite crackling, and there I found a stick of timber that Deacon Duncan had hewn, sae crooked that it could na lie still, but was thrashing about amang the trees. I tauld him that he must go and chain it doun, or it wad girdle the hail forest."

"Deacon Moore," he said, "made a ladder, and it was sae twisting, that before he got half way to the top he was on the under side, *looking up.*"

‡ The first male child born in Londonderry.

and generous in the extreme, but unfortunately possessed, what is too often the curse of superior endowments, a violent temper, and a want of self-control, which led sometimes to intemperance. To crown his misfortunes he had a wife who, in all but his bad qualities, was the opposite to himself. A separation took place, and he died in Vermont about the year '78· The second and third mechanics were William Cochran and James Houston, both blacksmiths. From these small beginnings we have gone on till now there is hardly a product of the mechanic arts, belonging either to the comforts or elegancies of life, which may not here be furnished.

The first use made of our water 'privileges* was for a saw and grist-mill, on the spot where the Peterborough Factory now stands. It was built by Jonathàn Morison, in 1751. This was an important event to the neighboring towns, who for several years brought all their grain to this mill. It was built for William Gordan, of Dunstable, Mass., and passed through several owners into the hands of Samuel Mitchell in 1759. The grist-mill was usually tended by his wife, and it was thought could hardly be a source of much profit; for she would take no toll from the poor, and when her customers were there at meal time, she would constrain them to partake of her fare, and often to remain through the night. The second saw-mill, where a saw and grist-mill now stands near the South Factory, was built by Thomas Morison in 1758, and the grist-mill added in 1770. The race-way to these mills is through a ledge of a sort of trap rock, on which it is extremely difficult to make any impression by blasting with gunpowder. Besides, the use of gunpowder for blasting seems to have been unknown here at that time. Large fires were therefore built upon the ledge, and when it was heated, water was thrown on. This scaled or cracked the rocks, all that was loosened was removed, and the same process repeated till a sufficient depth was gained.†

---

* For a very full and exact account of this part of the subject, see in the Appendix, the reports prepared by John H. Steele.

† There are now in town 6 grist-mills and 7 saw-mills.

At this period, (1770,) log-huts were little used; substantial frame-houses, many of them two stories high, had been erected; * and though hard labor and a homely fare were their portion, our people perhaps enjoyed as much then of the real comforts of life as at any subsequent period. Robust health, and confirmed habits of industry and exposure, enabled them to enjoy what would now be esteemed intolerable hardships. Four bridges had been built across our two principal streams; † the roads had greatly improved; there were no longer apprehensions of danger from the Indians or wild animals. I cannot well picture to myself happier domestic scenes than might then be found in one of those spacious kitchens which some of us have seen, though not in their glory. The kitchen stretched nearly across the house, — at one end was the ample *dresser*, filled up with pewter platters and basins of every size, all shining bright, and telling many a story to the beholder, of savory broths, ‡ and indian puddings, and possibly of pumpkin pies, even. The fire-place, which seemed to reach through half the length of the room, and was four or five feet high, not only contained between its capacious jambs, logs two or three feet in diameter, and almost sled length, heaped one above the other, with the proper accompaniments of foresticks and small wood; but back in one corner was an oven big enough to receive the largest pots and pans in which beans and brown bread ever were baked; and in both corners under the chimney was room for benches, where the children might sit on a winter's evening, parching corn, while the huge green back-log and back-stick were simmering and singing, and three or four little wheels with

* Hugh Wilson moved into the first two-story house in 1753. The first brick house was built by Nathan Richardson in 1811 or '12; the second by Jonas Loring in 1815. The whole number now in town is 23.

† The first near the great bridge in 1755; the second across Goose-brook previous to 1760; one at the North, and one at the South Factory in 1765, by labor from the town.

‡ Broth (barley or corn) was the favorite food. It is said that one of our eminent men, when a boy, wished that he could only be a king, for then he might have broth every day and as much as he wished.

various tones, were joining in the concert; and the large cat upon the wide stone hearth, interrupted occasionally by a gruff look from the dog, was industriously purring out her part of the accompaniment. There by the blazing fire, (for it would have been extravagance to burn any other light,) the children sit, with attention divided between the stories and the corn, and the young people, stealing now and then a sly glance or joke at the expense of their elders, burst out often into a chorus of laughter as their fathers, with grotesque humor, narrate the hardships and strange adventures of their early settlement, or dwell upon their favorite theme, the wonders of the old country, and especially " the pre-eminence of Ireland," against which all their anger is now forgotten. At length the time for retiring has come ; apples * and cider, after taking their station for a time upon the hearth, are served up. And now (for the guests, though neighbors, are expected to remain till morning,) a candle is lighted, the big Bible is brought out ; the oldest man receives it with reverence, and after reading a chapter with a voice of peculiar and unaffected solemnity, all join in prayer, and the elder people withdraw. Now is the time for the young. No longer with suppressed laughter, but with loud and bois- terous merriment, the evening is prolonged. The call from the sleepers, whose slumbers they have broken, produces only a momentary check. How long they sit up nobody knows ; but before light the young men are gone, for they must spend the day in the woods. The common mode of neighborly visiting among the women, was to go in the morning, carrying with them, not unfrequently a mile or more, their little wheels, and returning before dark ; thus enjoying all the advantages of good fellowship without loss of time.

This period of quiet however was of short duration. The difficulties with England soon began. Our fathers were too

* The first apple tree in the town was set out by John Swan, and is still alive. Apples must have been seldom used in the way I have mentioned, so early as 1770. The first cider was made by Mrs. John Smith. The apples were pounded in a barley mortar, and pressed in a cheese press.

zealous in their love of liberty to remain indifferent spectators, at a time like that. They entered warmly into the dispute. Private feelings were merged in their anxiety for the public good. News of the Lexington battle fell upon them like a sudden trump from heaven, summoning them to the conflict. "We all set out," said one who was then upon the stage, "with such weapons as we could get; going like a flock of wild geese, we hardly knew why or whither." The word came to Capt. Thomas Morison at day-light, that the regulars were upon the road; — in two hours, with his son and hired man, he was on his way to meet them; they on foot, he on horseback with a large *baking* of bread, which had just been taken from the oven, in one end of the bag, and pork in the other. This is but a sample of the general spirit which spread through the town, among men and women. "I was willing," said an old lady, whom I was questioning about those times, her pale cheeks kindling as she spoke, "that my father and brothers should run their chance with the rest." "I will not taste your tea," said another woman this same day; "I would as soon drink a man's blood."

At the battle of Bunker-hill, though there could not have been more than seventy or eighty families in the town, twenty-two of our citizens were present, and seventeen actively engaged in the fight. The night after the battle information was brought to Maj. Wilson* who then commanded the company, that the British were advancing upon the American lines, and at break of day every able-bodied man in town, with such weapons as he could procure, was on the march. At Townsend, those who went on foot heard the result of the battle and returned; † and then the old men, who had sons in the battle, set out to

* This anecdote is told me by his grandson, Gen. James Wilson, of Keene, who had it from his father, James Wilson Esq., who was born in this town 1766, and died in Keene, January, 1839.

† The greater part however were on horseback, and proceeded as far as West Cambridge, where they broke into a large vacant house, and passed the night.

learn whether their children were yet living, and had acquitted themselves like men.

Seventeen days before the Declaration of Independence, the following resolution was signed by eighty-three of our citizens, which included all the strong men, except those who were in the army, and possibly one or two besides.

" In consequence of the Resolution of the Continental Congress, and to show our determination in joining our American brethren in arms, in defending the lives, liberties, and properties of the United Colonies :—

" We, the subscribers, do hereby solemnly engage and promise, that we will to the utmost of our power, at the risque of our lives and fortunes, with ARMS oppose the hostile proceedings of the British fleets and armies against the United Colonies."

It has always been a matter of wonder to the world how our American Congress, which had no legal authority, whose strongest enactment was nothing more than a recommendation, should dare to make the Declaration of Independence, and still more, be able to carry out their measures through a long and discouraging war. The secret of their success is contained in the resolution which I have just read. It was the spirit which pervaded the people in their individual capacity, that nerved their arm and gave them strength. It was the solemn engagement and promise of the people, " at the risque of their lives and fortunes, with ARMS, to oppose the hostile proceedings of the British fleets and armies," that enabled Congress to take and carry through those strong measures which have been the admiration of every student of history. And in privations and hardships, that school of stern and manly virtues, in which not only here, but throughout the United Colonies, men were brought up, may we not see the hand of God stretched out to provide them with courage to declare, and strength to maintain their rights ; — that while He was elsewhere raising up men to direct the councils and lead the armies of the nation, He was here, and in places like this, making ready the strong nerves, the hard muscles, the unflinching souls, to fight the battles that should set them free. "He found them in a desert land, and in the waste, howling wilderness; he led them about, he instructed them," and when the great day had come, through the discipline which he had imposed, they were found equal to their work.

It is impossible now to paint the anxieties which prevailed through this little town during the war. Their remoteness from the scene of action, while it lessened their dangers, by no means diminished their fears. Rumors of terrible defeats and slaughters, of victories that had never been gained, and battles that were not fought, swayed them back and forth with doubts more cruel than the worst uncertainty. They were constantly in the dreadful expectation and suspense that precedes the conflict, and tries the soul more sharply than the hottest fight. No stranger made his appearance, but the town was full of surmises, suspicions and strange reports. He must be stopt, examined, and when fairly gone, suspicions were again afloat. The sufferings of those left behind were greater than of those in the war. It is sufficient however to say, that our citizens nobly redeemed the pledge they had given at the commencement of hostilities. During the war there were no mobs against the tories, for there was not a man here who favored the British cause.

Of our political history I shall say little. The terms on which the original settlement was made, were such that no Provincial* meeting could be held, or vote passed " obliging any person to do any part towards supporting the gospel, building a meeting-house and bridges, clearing and repairing roads." The act of incorporation was passed January 17th, 1760. These corporate townships are a peculiar feature in our government, and, so far as I know, have received only from a single author† anything of the attention which is due to so important a subject. Townships, with their peculiar rights, sprang, as I suppose, from the form of church discipline which was originally introduced into New England. Being composed entirely of the people, they contain in themselves all the elements

---

* See petition for incorporation.   † De Tocqueville.

of a pure democracy, and exercise all the functions of a more extended government. They are the schools in which young men are educated for higher offices, and in which all may be taught their duty as citizens. But the great purpose which they answer is, that they serve as a barrier against the encroachments of the state and federal governments.

A great danger in every government is, the centralization of power. For this reason only, that which relates to the whole nation in its federal capacity should be placed in the hands of the general government; and only that which relates to the whole state should be placed in the hands of the state government. All that remains should be left with the towns, and as a matter of fact nine-tenths of the real effective legislation in New England is performed by the towns. They raise the taxes, support the schools, roads, bridges. The parts of our general government which tend most to the centralization of power, and from which we have most to apprehend, as they, more than all others, tend to corruption, are the revenue and Post Office departments. Now, were it not for our townships, the same influence which pervades those departments, would take to itself, as it does in Prussia, the control of our roads, our schools, of all the taxes that are raised; and there would be at the heart of the republic an accumulation of power, with which no government on earth can be safely trusted. To prevent this dangerous result, we have in the first place our state governments, and then, what is of far greater importance, our town governments, which hold in their own hands more than nine-tenths of the real power which, so far as they are concerned, belongs to government.

Our town government, from the commencement, has been efficient and liberal. The town meetings in old times were often stormy, and ended in small results.* At all times of great

* An old man returning many years since from town meeting was asked what had been doing. "O," said he, "there was George Duncan, he got up and spakit a while, and Matthew Wallace, he got up and talkit a while, and Matthew Gray, he got up and blathered a while; and then they dismissed the meeting." A fair account of many town meetings.

party warfare in national politics, the contest here has been warm; and it has been well for the town, that while the same party (the conservative) has prevailed in every severe trial, it has at all times been confronted by a large and respectable minority. The severity of the contest kept alive the interest, it obliged men to examine and to think; and though, when parties are nearly equal, the temptation to gain a momentary triumph by dishonest artifice is sometimes too great to be resisted, the consciousness on each side that they are closely watched and cannot escape detection and exposure, will, where higher considerations fail, make them peculiarly circumspect in their movements. While the strong character of our citizens has done much to make political contentions severe since the first formation of parties under the federal government; the nearly equal division of parties has done much to sharpen the intellects, and restrain, if it did not correct, purposes grossly unjust.*

The ministerial history of the town is the darkest page in our calendar; but those whose feelings might be injured are now gone, and it is time that the subject should be placed in its true light. A Presbyterian minister, by the name of Johnston, came with the first settlers, and tarried with them about a year. Another by the name of Harvey, whose wife was the first person laid in the old grave-yard, was here for a time. A Mr. Powers supplied the desk in 1764. This is all that we know of them. John Morison, of a family entirely distinct from our first settlers, was born at Pathfoot, in Scotland, May 22, 1743; was graduated at Edinburgh, February 17, 1765; arrived at Boston the May following, and was ordained at Peterborough, November 26, 1766. From all that I can learn he was a man of decided talents; but it must be borne in mind, that the same ability will appear always more conspicuous in a bad than in a good man, just as a horse, or a building of perfect symmetry will always appear smaller than another of the same dimensions

---

* Party spirit in politics, has perhaps in no town been more violent than here, but it has never been permitted to disturb the cordiality of social intercourse.

whose parts are out of proportion. But after making all due allowance, we must, I believe, conclude that Mr. Morison possessed more than common powers, for good or for evil. But soon he proved himself an intemperate, licentious man, dangerous alike as the companion of either sex. A charitable construction was put upon the first symptoms of intemperance. At a party he was found unable to walk, and it was necessary to take him through the room where the young people were collected, in order to place him upon a bed. This was managed with so much adroitness, that no suspicion was raised, except with three or four church-members who were disposed to view it as an accident, at a time when similar casualties were not uncommon. But soon, while his bad habits in this line became notorious, his evil passions in another direction flared out, to the general scandal of the town. A Presbytery was held ; he was suspended from his office for two or three months, a thing probably to his taste, as his salary was *not* suspended. At length, however, the people could no longer tolerate him ; he relinquished his connection with the society in March, 1772 ; visited South Carolina, returned and joined the American army at Cambridge in '75. He was present at Bunker-hill, but excused himself from entering the battle on the ground that his gun-lock was not in order. The next day he joined the British, and continued in some capacity with them till his death, which took place at Charleston, S. C., December 10, 1782. He became a professed atheist. It is said that he spent his last days, when he was daily sinking to the grave, among profligate, abandoned associates, taking his part in every species of dissipation which his decaying strength would permit ; and just before his death, gave a sum of money to his companions, requesting them to drink it out upon his coffin. His wife, Sarah Ferguson, in every respect a true, exemplary woman, never to the time of her death, (November, 1824, æt. 84,) lost either the interest or the confidence with which she had first joined her fortunes to his. It is refreshing to add, that their son, John Morison, who died more than forty years ago, was, by the uniform consent of all who knew him, one of the most pure-hearted and clear-headed men that our town has produced. I have never heard him mentioned by one who had known him except with strong affection and respect. He received his education at Exeter, where for a time he was also a teacher. When, many years after, I went to Exeter, and was there in a very humble employment, a friendless, ignorant boy, the fact that my name was the same with his, had, I have no doubt, a very considerable influence in bespeaking for me unusual kindness on the part of my employer,* who had been his early friend.

From '72 to '78 our people had no settled ministry. The meeting-house was built in '77, and traditions are handed down respecting a Mr. Clarke, who was preaching here at the time. Many who heard him testify that the following is nearly an exact account of the exordium to one of his discourses. "This is a stately house ; and who meet here? The folk, they meet here, and the Deil, he meet here too ; and he is amang the foremost and the fattest † o' ye. An' he 's peeking out at ye, like a wee mouse in the wa' ; ye dinna see him, but he kens ye. An' now where is the gun to shoot him wi' ? Here it is," said he, lifting up the Bible and taking aim, "here is the gun. *Too! too!* he 's deed, he 's deed." The preaching of that period was usually without notes, the sermons very ordinary, very long, and made up very much of repetitions, especially of a continual play upon the words of the text.

The second settled minister of the place, David Annan,‡ was born at Cupar of Fife in Scotland, April 4, 1754, came early to America, was educated at New Brunswick College, N. J., was ordained for Peterborough, at the call of the people

---

* Joseph Smith Gilman.

† This, it was thought, might apply to Dea. Mitchell and his wife, as he was usually foremost, and she the fattest in the assembly.

‡ His brother, Robert Annan, was first at Wallkill, N. Y., then pastor of the Federal Street Church in Boston, then of a society in Philadelphia, where he died. He was a man of uncommon power and of great austerity.

here, by the Presbytery which met at Wallkill, N. Y., October, 1778, and was dismissed from this society at his own request, by the Presbytery of Londonderry, at their June session here, in 1792. He was deposed from the ministry by the Presbytery of Londonderry in 1800, and died in Ireland in 1802. The people received him with high expectations, and were slow to believe anything against him. Though in talents inferior to his predecessor, he was a man of more than common endowments, but was intemperate and morose, uniting in his character the extremes, which sometimes meet in smaller tyrants than Nero, of levity and cruelty. With the elders of the church he was stern, inflexible, and austere. With young men his conversation was loose, licentious, corrupt. He was easily flattered, but being opposed, haughty and overbearing. When *treated to toddy* at a public house by a man of no good repute, he expressed himself delighted with his companion, and wished he had a whole church like him ; and when one of the most upright of his society* attempted in private and with great kindness to remonstrate with him on his conduct, his only reply was, "It is a wise people that can instruct their minister ; " " and a foolish minister," it might have been rejoined, " who cannot be instructed by his people." Rev. Mr. Miles, of Temple, used to relate, that once on coming to his house to exchange with him, he found him sitting at a table with a fiddle, (made by his own hands,) a bottle of rum and a Bible before him. In his own house he was the severest of tyrants. His wife, an amiable, discreet, patient, uncomplaining woman, often retired at night amid actions and threats, which left to her scarcely a hope that her life would be spared till morning, and sometimes she passed the whole night with her children in the woods. After the birth of their last child his conduct towards her and her children was so brutal that it could no longer be borne. She fled from his house with her child,

---

* Henry Ferguson, a thoroughly excellent man. Not one of the name is now among us. Three of the sons removed to South Carolina, where the last of them, having accumulated a large property, died within a few years.

and a petition for a bill of divorce, on the ground of extreme cruelty, was granted at once by the court with a feeling almost of horror at the disclosures then made.

The only organized mob, of which I find any evidence in our history, was against Mr. Annan. Just at the time of his wife's flight with her child, when stories were spread through the town, and every one was burning with indignation, the young men who were collected at a ball, talking over the circumstances till they had wrought themselves into a perfect rage, determined to take the matter into their own hands. Blacking their faces with soot, disguising themselves in every uncouth dress, and provided with a rough spruce pole, at the dead of night, in the autumn of 1799, they knocked at the door of Mr. Annan's house, and when he, suspecting no harm, came to them as if from his bed, three * of the strongest among them seized him, placed him upon the pole, and the whole party with shouting and howling, the tinkling of cow-bells, the blowing of horns and pumpkin vines, carried him a full half mile and threw him into a muddy pond. An attempt was made by Mr. Annan, who always after went armed with pistols, to bring the rioters to justice. Writs were issued against them, and had he possessed a single friend, he might have succeeded. But nothing could be proved; the feelings of those who had been most severe against him began to relent, and they looked with pity on the solitary, friendless, dejected old man.

The provocation in this case undoubtedly was great. But never, we may safely say, in a well organized society, can an emergency arise where individuals may be justified in taking upon themselves that which it belongs to the natural retributions of Providence and the authorised laws of the land to inflict. It may pain and vex us to see the oppressor go untouched; but sooner or later punishment will overtake him, and we know

---

* " What do ye want o' me ?" he inquired sternly. " Only a little of your good company," was the reply from a young man, whose name has since been known through the United States.

not how severely he may suffer at the very moment when he seems most happy.

Mr. Morison and Mr. Annan were the only settled ministers in the place for fifty years. Two questions naturally come up: How could such men be tolerated so long; and how could religion be kept alive under such instructions?

They were tolerated, in the first place, because of the great veneration which was then attached to the profession. "Ministers," said one at the commencement of the difficulties with Mr. Morison, "are edged tools, and we maun aye be carefu' how we handle them." "Keep yoursel' to yoursel'," said an elder of the church with great solemnity to his son, who was beginning to intimate that Mr. Annan was not what he should be. Another reason which made many, and those among the most rigid disciplinarians, more tolerant than they would otherwise have been was, that the ministers though wrong in practice were yet sound in faith; and error in belief was esteemed far more dangerous than in heart or life. This doctrine of antinomianism was then carried to a degree of extravagance which finds no sympathy now. An illustration may be given. A Mr. Taggart, one of the straightest in faith, but who was intemperate in his habits, had a remarkable gift in prayer, and this gift was rather increased than diminished by the exhilaration of ardent spirits. At funerals, where there was no minister, he was usually called upon to pray; and sometimes when unable to stand, would kneel by his chair and edify the assembly by the readiness and fervor of his devotions. Henry Ferguson once met him lying in the road, and after helping him up told him that this conduct was inconsistent with his place in the church. "Ah," said he, "but we are not our own keepers." Sometime after, Mr. Ferguson was nominated an elder, and Mr. Taggart, on the strength of this conversation, publicly opposed him as a man who trusted entirely to works. These two reasons in their influence upon some of our own people, and still more upon the Presbyteries with which they were connected, together with the personal influence of Robert

Annan, who was a strong man in the church, will sufficiently account for the long infliction upon the patience and moral feelings of the community.

The next question, how could religion be kept alive under such circumstances, is readily answered. Our people were always readers, and the Bible was almost their only book. Here they went for counsel and support. It was to them prophet, and priest. With all their reverence for the public ministrations of religion, their reverence for the written word was far greater. In the next place, the practice of family prayer was faithfully observed. Morning and evening the Scriptures were read; and if the flame of devotion burnt dim in the house of public worship, it was not permitted to go out upon the family altar. Besides, they had preachers more powerful than man. They were strangers in a strange land; in the midst of perpetual alarms and dangers; sickness, death, and all the vicissitudes of life entered their dwellings in the wilderness, and through its loneliness spoke to them as they never can speak in a more cultivated place. They had before coming here been well imbued with the principles of religion; and besides, the human soul is so constituted, that it cannot live and be at peace without a religious faith. Rites and ordinances are an important means of advancing the cause of religion. But they are not all. God has never left himself without witness among men. The success of his word does not rest upon a mortal priesthood. Religion is an essential want of the soul, deeply fixed in its nature. Men may stifle its cravings, may for a time suppress them, and unhallowed servants at the altar may help to keep them down. But they cannot be destroyed until the soul itself is crushed. Religion, dishonored by its ministers, degraded by the false ideas that have gathered round it, can never be banished so long as these human hearts, beating with hopes, anxieties and fears, look round upon a world of change and weakness, and find nowhere here the object that fills up their wants.

The church thus far had been Presbyterian. After Mr. Annan left, the late Rev. Zephaniah Swift Moore was invited to remain, but declined, not wishing to settle as a Presbyterian. After he left, a paper * was handed round and signed by all, or nearly all, the church, expressing a willingness to settle Mr. Moore in the Congregational form ; but he, in the mean time, had found another place ; and the town continued without a settled minister till Oct. 23, 1799, when Rev. Elijah Dunbar was ordained. Originally the church had belonged to the Londonderry Presbytery. At the settlement of Mr. Annan, by his request, it received a dismission from this and joined the New-York Presbytery. When Mr. Dunbar was settled, that Presbytery had become extinct, and the church here was left an independent body. It then adopted the Congregational form, and though there were still some who preferred the Presbyterian mode, all attended upon his ministry, with the understanding however that once a year the communion should be administered by a Presbyterian, and in the Presbyterian manner. For many years the Rev. Dr. Wm. Morison, of Londonderry, administered the ordinance every autumn. It was always a day of uncommon interest ; the house was crowded ; and though but a child when he last came, I well remember the solemnity and awe with which I was impressed by the countenance, accent, and manner of that aged and faithful minister of Christ. Mr. Dunbar, with unsullied character, remained the minister of the town till June 19, 1822, when a portion of his people who had never liked the Congregational form, and others who had never been quite at ease under an Armenian preacher, withdrew and formed the Presbyterian Society. Mr. Dunbar continued pastor of the Congregational Society, till Feb. 1827. He was succeeded in June of the same year, by Rev. Abbot, D.D. who had preached in town a short time, thirty years before, and who is still the pastor.

The Presbyterian church was built in 1825, about half a mile north of the old meeting-house, and during the present year has been removed to the village. Rev. Peter Holt was installed pastor March, 1827, and resigned March, 1835.—

* This paper, I understand, is now with Dea. Jonathan Smith.

Rev. Mr. Pine was installed June, 1836, and dismissed Jan. 1837. Rev. Joshua Barret was pastor from Feb. 1837 till Feb. 1839.

The Baptist church was constituted, Nov., 1822, containing forty members. Rev. Charles Cummings was the first pastor. Rev. Mr. Goodnow, from June, 1831 ; Rev. George Daland, from March 1834 till 1836 ; Rev. John Peacock, one year from Sept., 1837, have been the ministers. Rev. J. M. Willmorth, the present pastor, was settled Sept., 1838.

There has been for some years a Methodist Society ; and the Universalists have sometimes had preaching in the Congregational meeting-house.

Of our public schools, important and vitally connected as they are with all the better prospects of our country, my limits will allow me to say but little. From 1760 till 1797, the annual appropriations were small, never more than one hundred dollars, seldom fifty dollars, and often nothing. I do not find that any school-houses were erected by the town, before 1790, when the town was divided into five districts, and provision made for the erection of five buildings.* From 1797 to 1805, three hundred dollars were annually raised for schools, except in 1801, when the appropriation was but two hundred dollars. From 1805 to 1808, four hundred dollars were raised annually ; and since then the town has uniformly raised what the law required, and, I believe, no more, except that for a few years past one half the literary fund (about seventy-five dollars per annum) has been given to aid the feeble districts. The school tax now, (and it has not materially varied for several years,) is eight hundred and eighty-one dollars and thirty-six cents.

The condition of the schools, public and private, during the last, and the first twenty years of the present century, was de-

* There were school-houses long before this, which had been erected by neighborhoods. In the same way schools also were supported. The public appropriations give a wrong idea of what has actually been paid for this purpose. The sum now paid for private schools is at least equal to what is paid by the town. There are now in town eleven districts, each with a brick school-house.

cidedly bad. Some improvement has been made since then ; and great credit is due to the spirited exertions of a few individuals in different parts of the town. Still, (for I should pervert the purposes of this day, if I stood here only to flatter or to praise,) *the subject has not received the attention which its importance demands, and our public schools do not take the place that we should expect, from the general intelligence of our citizens.* They are peculiarly the property and province of the whole people, by whom they live and prosper, and without whose hearty assistance and co-operation, committees and teachers can accomplish nothing. All who take an interest in the welfare of their children or of society, will not be slow to do what can be done for these, the true nurseries of a nation's mind. They will not grudge to the teacher his hard earned pay, nor forget to do at home, that which alone can render his labors easy and effective.

Our Libraries demand a moment's attention. There had been previously a library of a similar character ; but as early as 1811 the Peterborough Social Library was got up, containing not far from one hundred volumes. So judicious a selection I have never seen. There was hardly a book which did not deserve its place. I well remember the astonishment with which, at the age of eleven, I first looked on what seemed to me such an immense collection of books ; nor can I soon forget the uniform kindness with which my early reading was encouraged, and in some measure directed by the librarian, Daniel Abbot. In an intellectual point of view, I look back on no period of my life with so much satisfaction, as on the two years when, at the age of fourteen and fifteen, I lived with Samuel Templeton, as honest a man as this or any town has ever produced. During the hour which he always gave me at noon, and in the evening by fire-light, I read the standard histories in our language, and made myself acquainted with the important events of the ancient world. When a volume was finished, I would set out at dark, after a hard day's work, walk three miles to the village, and, enriched with a new treasure, would return almost unmindful of the woods and their near vicinity to the grave-yard and old meeting-house, which especially on a wintry autumnal night, standing there naked, black, and lonely, was, as I know full well, a fearful object enough to a child. The Peterborough Social Library became gradually neglected, and was sold about 1830, when a new library on the same plan was got up, and contains now about three hundred volumes. The Union and Phœnix Factories have each a library of about one hundred and fifty volumes. The Ministerial Library, (an excellent institution,) contains five hundred, and the public town library about nine hundred volumes ; so that, besides private collections, there are now in town for the use of readers two thousand volumes.

One word let me here say to the young. These schools and libraries are for you. All that is most valuable in education is within your reach. Many have been the bitter but unavailing regrets of those, who, despising these precious advantages in youth, have found themselves, as men and women, ignorant and incompetent to the great duties that were before them. The busiest day has intervals of rest, and he who is in earnest for knowledge will receive it. Let your leisure moments be sacredly devoted to the improvement of your minds. You might not covet the honors of a professional life, if you knew its painful watchings, anxieties and toils ; but as you value the esteem of others, or your own happiness, as you would do your part to carry on the progress of the world, as you would be useful and respected in manhood, and escape a leafless, neglected, old age, do not fail now, while the time is, to use every means that is held out for your intellectual advancement.

Another subject of much interest in our history I can but just sketch out. Early in our history, the hand-card, the little wheel, and the loom with the hand-shuttle, were almost the only instruments of manufacture in the place. The grandmother of Governor Miller paid for four hundred acres of land in fine linen, made entirely (except getting out the flax) by her own hands. With the exception of hats and the wedding

5

gown, which was usually of satin, and handed down as a sort of heir-loom to children and grand-children, even (three genera- tions not unfrequently being married in the same dress) all the articles of clothing were manufactured at home. There the wool was carded, spun, woven, colored, and made up into gar- ments. The hides were indeed sent away to be tanned; but the same hides were brought home as leather, and the shoe- maker came always to the house with his bench, lasts and awls. To use foreign goods was considered, as indeed it was, great extravagance. After the first store was opened here, in 1771, one hundred pounds of butter was the price usually paid for a calico gown. Almost every article of food and clothing was then prepared at home. The first clothier's shop for taking in wool to card and cloth to dress, was built by William Powers, in 1780, and this was the only factory in town till 1793; when, on the spot now occupied by the Phœnix factory, "a* wooden building two hundred feet long, and two stories high, was erected by Samuel Smith, and was the wonder of the whole country. Mr. Smith had in this building a paper-mill, a saw-mill, an oil- mill, a clothier's shop, a trip-hammer shop, a wool-carding ma- chine, and a dwelling-house." This bold step gave the first de- cided impulse to the manufacturing enterprise of the place. It brought into notice the great water privileges that were here possessed. The first cotton factory for the manufacture of yarn was started in 1810. And from that time to this, one after another place has been taken up, until the capital vested in and upon the different water privileges, — not forgetting the peg-mill in which twenty-five hundred bushels of shoe-pegs are made annually, — is now estimated at three hundred thousand dollars; the cotton factories alone producing annually one million seven hundred and twenty-five thousand yards of cloth; and the amount of property annually imported and sold in our stores, it is estimated, cannot be less than seventy-five thousand dollars.

* I have received from John H. Steele, Esq. a very full and exact account of all our manufacturing establishments from the beginning, which, in a con- densed form, may be found in the Appendix.

With this change there has been a great influx of people from abroad ; the habits and pursuits of the town have undergone an important revolution.*

But with all this show of enterprise and prosperity there is danger. Our young women, the future mothers, who are to form the character of the next generation, are not educated as their mothers were, at home, in comparative solitude, where the mind had leisure to mature, and the affections to expand, but are taken from their homes, work together in large companies, and board in crowded houses. It is surely a solemn responsibility that rests upon the owners and agents of these establishments. Thus far, their conduct has been marked by generosity and high principle. But it is well for all to be awake ; for the operatives to remember that they have rights and duties for themselves beyond the mere comforts and luxuries of an animal life. They have minds, they have hearts which require to be clothed and fed, and unless now in season they provide for their intellectual, moral and spiritual wants, for the support of a refined intelligence, a modest but true moral independence, we shall repent the day that has clothed our bodies with improved garments, but left us with inferior minds, — with souls robbed of their pure affections, lofty freedom, and immortal hopes.

The notice of our early history would be incomplete without some scattered facts of a different character. Our ancestors, with all the rest of the world, believed in the bodily manifestation of the devil, in the existence of witches, and the appearance of ghosts. It is not my purpose to do any thing more than relate what they believed. A small, lean, aged woman, by the name of Stinson, was uniformly regarded as a witch. A cat somewhere in town was observed to act strange-

* A Post-Office was established in town, about 1790; John Smith was the first Post-Master. A Mr. Balch first carried the mail. He was succeeded by Asa Gibbs, who for many years rode on horseback from Portsmouth to Brattleborough once a week. At last he rode in a little wagon and carried a few passengers. He was killed in 1824, by falling from a bridge. He was succeeded by his son. Stages began to run in 1826 or '27, and now a daily stage each way is crowded with passengers.

ly, hot water was thrown upon her, and straightways Mrs. Stinson's back was dreadfully afflicted with the St. Anthony's fire. On another occasion, a good man near Sharon shot at a crow many times, but the bird only flew round and laughed at him. He at last took off a silver sleeve-button, and with it broke the crow's wing; whereupon Mrs. Stinson was found with a lame arm. At her funeral, which was about fifty years ago, though she was hardly more than a skeleton, the strong men who bore her to the grave were almost crushed to the earth by the weight of sin, and their shoulders remained for weeks black and blue.

There was also one Hannah Scott, who supposed herself bewitched by an old woman named Aspy, of Hancock. The girl lay more than a month without the power of opening her eyes any more than she could open a part of her cheek. While in this state, she could tell exactly who were passing, how they looked, what they had with them, and what was going on in different houses, and in different parts of the town. She always said that if old Aspy would come and bless her she should recover. The witch came, and passing her hands over the girl's forehead, with the words, " your God bless you and my God bless you," ended the charm. This, it will be seen at once, is but the counterpart of what has recently taken place under the name of Animal Magnetism.

All this was religiously believed. And we in our day have known one* who, to his dying hour, firmly believed that he had twice been honored by a personal interview with the devil. Old Baker — what child in Peterborough within the last sixty years has not danced to his fiddle, with an ecstasy which no other music ever gave? Who does not remember the benevo-

* Baker Moore, a colored man, born in Boston, 1755, bought as a slave and brought to this town by Deacon Moore, in 1763. At the age of twenty-two, he purchased his freedom for two hundred dollars, which he never felt obliged to pay, nor was it exacted. He died January, 1839. There have been in this town eight slaves; two, Baker and Rose, belonging to Deacon Moore; two to David Steele; two to Samuel Aulds; one to Isaac Mitchell; one to Captain Robbe. There may possibly have been others.

lent, complacent smile with which his honest black face and white teeth and eyes shone, as raising his instrument to his chin, and producing the first sweet notes, he looked about on the delighted children that were listening or romping round him? But when we knew him, " the minstrel was infirm and old," and now he is gone — light may the turf rest upon his bosom. Such men are like fossil remains and petrifactions, which preserve the exact lineaments of plants and animals centuries perhaps after the living species has become extinct. , Their minds receive in youth the impressions then current, and there remain fixed through life ; so that Baker in these matters may be considered a fair sample of the belief which prevailed sixty or seventy years ago. It was seldom that he could be induced to speak upon the subject, and then with symptoms of terror, which it would be difficult to describe. I remember, however, to have heard him once, after casting round a fearful look to be sure that the doors were shut, and the evil spirit not actually in the room. As he was driving the cows to pasture, he said, one evening he met a man who very kindly accosted him, and in the course of the conversation told his fortune, mentioning things that no mortal could have known. He gave him a book, with the request that he would read it. Baker took the book ; but it hung like lead upon his spirits. He carried it constantly with him, for he was afraid to leave it behind, and at last having met " the man" again on horseback, in the northwest part of the town, he returned the book ; whereupon the man's eyes glistened like fire, his cloven foot appeared, and he was terribly angry. Baker looked up a moment after and he was gone. All this, our good friend as much believed as he believed in his own existence, and it is but a fair sample of what our fathers also believed. One man, William M'Nee, had horse-shoe nails driven into the horns of all his cattle, to save them from the witches, and it was generally believed that horse-shoes, witch-hazel rods, and silver, were effectual securities against their influence.

Another singular fact may be here added, to illustrate this

part of their character. Wm. Robbe, — his mother was always supposed to have saved the life of the elder Wm. Smith, by sucking the wound made by a poisonous snake in Lunenburg, and both he and his parents were modest, excellent people,— Wm. Robbe was a seventh son ; and it was generally thought that certain diseases could be cured by him. He was not a quack ; — receiving pay destroyed the charm. He gave a small silver coin to those who came. The visits became so numerous, that he left the town in consequence, and went to Stoddard ; but being unfortunate there, was obliged to return and bear the onerous duties which the accident of being the seventh son imposed upon him. The belief in his power was general, and borne out by reputed facts, which we cannot here stop to examine or even specify.

I would now speak of the characteristics of our inhabitants.

In the first place they have been always distinguished for their mental activity, and love of knowledge. The original emigrants from Ireland were by no means an ignorant people. They were brought up in the common school education of the day, and most of them were imbued with the religious education then more common in Scotland and the North of Ireland, than in the sister kingdom of England. What was wanting in outward instruction, was, in some measure, supplied by their own intellectual energy and zeal. The respect which has always been paid to learning, may in part be understood from the number and character of our educated men. Twenty-eight* have graduated at

---

* Jeremiah Smith, 1781; James Wilson, 1789; Walter Little, 1796; John Wilson, 1799; Stephen Mitchell, 1802; John Stuart, 1803; William Ritchie, 1804; Stephen P. Steele, 1808; Charles J. Stuart, 1809; David Steele, 1810; James Porter, 1810; Jonathan Steele, 1811; Isaac P. Osgood, 1814; Jesse Smith, 1814; David Steele, 1815; Joseph Brackett, Jonathan Smith, 1819; James Wilson, 1820; Albert Smith, 1825; Josiah Ballard, John H. Morison, 1831; Robert Wilson, 1832; Artemas L. Holmes, 1835; Solomon Laws, 1836; Horace Morison, 1837; Nath'l Holmes, 1837; Nath'l H. Morison, 1839; Bernard B. Whittemore, 1839.

The above list, in which one or two may possibly be omitted, has been kindly furnished me by S. P. Steele, Esq. Others not born here, have gone to College from this place, as Dr. Reuben D. Mussey.

our different colleges. James Wilson, for a time Representative in Congress, and Jonathan Steele, a Judge of the Supreme Court, were widely known. Nor must we omit the name of Jesse Smith, who having graduated at Dartmouth College in 1814, studied medicine with Dr. George C. Shattuck, of Boston, and afterwards established himself in Cincinnati, where as a professer in the Medical College and a practitioner, he stood decidedly at the head of his profession. He died of the Cholera in 1833, universally lamented, having fallen a victim to his humane and fearless exertions for the suffering, during the ravages of that frightful pestilence.

Among the educated sons of Peterborough, is another, yet happily numbered with the living, who was your first choice for the task which I am now laboring to perform. I cannot but regret that it was out of his power to accept your call ; for there is no man alive so intimately acquainted with our history, or so well able to do justice to the character of our people. He was born November 29, 1759 ; — his father, William Smith, perhaps the best educated of our early settlers, and who was a delegate to the Provincial Congress in 1774, was a man of singular discretion, modesty and goodness ; and his mother, (the daughter of John Morison,) was a driving, energetic woman. He was one of seven sons, * all (except one who died before his strength was brought out,) uncommon men. Until recently, for the last sixty years, they have had here an influence possessed by no other family, and have done more than any others to form the character and advance the prosperity of the town. Seventy years ago, if we may trust to one who then knew them well, a more rude, uncouth, impudent set of boys was not to be found in Peterborough. Very early, however, Jeremiah's enthusiastic love of knowledge began to act. But the facilities for learning within his reach, were greatly inferior to what may now be enjoyed by the poorest and most neglected child among us. There were no books to be had ; and the

* Robert, John, William, James, Jeremiah, Jonathan, and Samuel.

schools were wretched.   I have heard him speak of going, when a small boy, three or four miles to procure the loan of some ordinary volume, and the tears of disappointment with which he often came away from his teacher's blundering explanation of subjects which he was longing to understand.   But never yet did the youth, urged on by an unquenching desire to know, stop short through outward obstructions.   They only quicken his zeal, and give new energy to his powers.   So was it with our townsman.   At the age of twelve he began to study Latin at the public school, which was then kept in the old meeting-house by Master Rudolphus Greene.   After this he studied for a short time with a Mr. Donovan at New-Boston, and then with Rev. Mr. Emerson, of Hollis, where he began Greek, and finished his preparation for college.   He entered Harvard College in 1777.   Just at this time he enlisted for two months in the service, was present at the battle of Bennington, where a portion of his gun was shot off in his hands, and a musket-ball grazing his throat, left its mark there for many years.   He left Cambridge in 1779, and was graduated at Rutgers College, N. J., in 1781.   He now began the study of the law in Barnstable, 1782 '83 ; spending after this a year at Andover and two years in Salem ; filling at each place the office of teacher in connection with his studies.

He began to practice here as a lawyer in 1787, was a member of our legislature three years ; during which time he revised the laws of the State.   Previous to this time, Peterborough had been notorious for its lawsuits, and furnished no small portion of the whole litigation of the county.   These foolish disputes he always discountenanced ; sometimes cooling down his angry client by pleasantry, and sometimes dissuading him by more serious considerations.   It was the opinion of our most intelligent people at the time, that the town might afford to pay Jerry Smith five hundred dollars a year, simply for his influence in preventing lawsuits.

But a wider field was opening.   In 1791, he was chosen a representative to Congress.   To this office he was appointed at four successive elections, and continuing in it through nearly the whole of Washington's Administration, he resigned during the Presidency of the elder Adams, after the May session of 1797. Here it was his privilege to become acquainted with the great men of the time; with Washington, with John Adams, with Jefferson and Madison, with John Jay, John Marshall, Samuel Dexter, and Fisher Ames, during the interesting period when the French revolution was breaking out with the suddenness of a new volcano. Upon leaving Congress, he was appointed United States Attorney for the District of New Hampshire, and soon after, while holding this office, was made Judge of Probate for the county of Rockingham, having in the mean-time removed to Exeter. In 1801, he was appointed Judge of the Circuit Court of the United States, and during a part of the year 1802, was at the same time Judge of Probate, Judge of the United States District Court, and Chief-Justice of the Supreme Court of New Hampshire. He continued Chief-Justice till 1809, when he was chosen Governor of the State. He returned to the bar in 1810 ; in 1813 was again made Chief-Justice, and continued in this office till 1816, when he withdrew from public life. In 1820, he gave up his practice at the bar. It is not my purpose, nor am I competent to speak of the ability, learning, uprightness, and independence with which the duties of these high, various, and responsible offices were dis-charged. His acts, are they not written in the Chronicles, and themselves an important part of the public history, of our State? The assaults of party violence are over ; and they who were once the most earnest to assail, are now among the fore-most to acknowledge his intellectual vigor, great learning, and above all the spotless purity of his character as a public man. It is not for such as me to praise or censure him. The verdict has been made up by his peers ; and if they are to be trusted, his name will be handed down as one of the two most able and accomplished public men that New Hampshire, during the first two centuries of her political existence, has produced.

In this our great family meeting, may we not indulge in the expression of personal feeling ? Especially may not a younger brother speak of what he owes to one full of honors as of years, whose heart is with us though he be not here? From my childhood up, I have been the creature of kindness, and should I die with the consciousness of having done no other good than to have called out the kind acts which have been extended to myself, I shall go down to the grave feeling that I have not lived in vain. There are others towards whom the fullness of my gratitude can be known only by the Searcher of all hearts. But for them, I should not now be among the living. What I should have been without him I almost tremble to think. Just standing upon the verge of life, with principles unformed, with a yearning indeed for knowledge, which had followed me like some mystic spell from my earliest recollections, hoping and yet despairing, with no claim but inexperience and helplessness, I received from him all the kindness that a father could give. Dull indeed must I have been, if I have not profited from the richness of his mind and the advantages which his aid has placed within my reach.

I have dwelt on this example, not for the purpose of gratifying private feelings, but because it is the brightest illustration that our town has furnished to the young, of a really great intellect, strengthened and adorned by a finished education. When I see such a man, and feel his strength of mind, the richness and variety of his intellectual stores, his vivacity and wit, and, more than all, his utter scorn for everything mean or dishonest, I forget the offices through which he has passed. They have borrowed much, but added little to the dignity of the man. And the elements which have made him what he is, belong peculiarly to the Peterborough mind, and may be seen, less clearly developed indeed, in many of our citizens.

But while the intellect of our people is shewn in the number and character of educated men that have gone from among them, it is shewn still more in their general character. I might select many among those whom I have personally known, who, if not polished so as to bring out all the shades and rich veins of intellect, have yet been sufficiently cultivated to shew minds capable of grasping strong thoughts, and acting upon the most important interests of public and private life.   Many excel them in every species of intellectual refinement, in the taste for poetry, the fine arts, and the niceties of literature.   But in sterling good sense, in close and severe reasoning, in solid infor- mation, especially an acquaintance with the standard works of history, theology, and some branches of philosophy, the people of few towns are superior, if indeed, as a whole, they are equal to those who have lived here for the last twenty or thirty years. Like every place, it has those who recognise no such thing as purely intellectual tastes and wants.   But thanks be to heaven they are few, and their influence in the town has been only to make men shun their example.   Our young men, kindling with nobler hopes, look to other quarters for instruction.

The next remarkable feature of our town during the past century, has been courage.   It was shewn by our fathers in Ireland, and has not deserted their sons.   As a people they have never shrunk from peril.   At the first sound of danger, their custom has been to fly to the scene of action.   So was it in the Indian and French wars, in which, when there were not in town more than forty families, six of our citizens were slain in a single day.*   So was it after the news of the battle of Lexington.   Of the seventeen engaged at Bunker- hill, one man (John Graham, remarkable for his skill in throw- ing stones) after exhausting his ammunition, unwilling to retire, seized upon stones and hurled them, not without effect, against the enemy ; another (John Taggart) after fighting as long as it was possible to fight, in the retreat stopped his companions while yet in the midst of danger, and when they had refreshed themselves from their canteens, exclaimed, " Neu let us trust in God and tak the tother run."   Randal M'Alester was severely shot through the neck ; Thomas Green, in a fainting and almost expiring state was saved by his friend Gilchrist, who carried him on his back from Bunker-hill to Medford.   Lieutenant (after- wards Captain) William Scott, early in the action had one of

* In a ranging company commanded by Robert Rogers, in 1757. See Farmer's Belknap.

the bones of his leg broken just below the knee. He continued coolly paring musket balls and handing them to his soldiers. He was among the very hindmost in the retreat, when he received in his thigh and the lower part of his body four additional balls, and, bleeding at nine orifices, fainted upon the field. When he came to himself, a British soldier was standing over him, with his bayonet, and asked, with an oath if he did not deserve to be killed. "I am in your power," was the reply, "and you can do with me as you please." He was rescued by a British officer and permitted to remain unmolested upon the field through that cold frosty night. The next morning he was taken to Boston, and thence to Halifax, where he was imprisoned. With a gimblet, a bayonet, and an old knife, furnished by a friend without,* he, and six of his companions broke the prison, and by the help of that same friend got on board a vessel and reached home the following August. He set out immediately for the American army which he joined on Long Island, was taken with two thousand others at the capture of Fort Washington ;† but the night after, tying his sword to the back of his neck and his watch to his hat-band, he swam a mile and a half to Fort Lee upon the Jersey shore, eluding the vigilance of the British frigate, that had been stationed there to guard the prisoners. He continued in the army till after the retreat of Lafayette before Cornwallis, and from that time was engaged upon the ocean.

The same intrepidity which he had shewn in war continued in peace. The following is from the Boston Independent Chronicle of July 12, 1792, under the head of news from Philadelphia, July 2. After stating in general terms a terrific tempest that occurred the day before, and some of the accidents caused by it, they add ; " Since writing the above account, we

* John Morison, Esq. the brother of Thomas and Jonathan. He lived in Nova-Scotia, was a Whig, and like others of the family not being able to keep his opinions to himself, became suspected, fled from the British Provinces and lived for a time in Peterborough.

† November 16, 1776. See Holmes's Annals of America, Vol II, p. 251.

further learn that a boat from this city to the Jersey shore, was overset within fifty rods of Samuel Cowper's wharf. There were in the boat Captain Scott, Mr. Blake, his wife and four small children, a young woman and Mr. Betis — in all nine persons—none of whom could swim but Captain Scott. The Captain by the most astonishing and praiseworthy exertions, was able, providentially, to save them all. He swam ashore with one child hanging to his neck and one to each arm, and he returned to the boat amidst the boisterous waves raging in a furious and frightful manner, and brought the others, who had with much difficulty held by the boat, safe to land."

The editor of the Boston paper adds: " For the honor of Captain Scott, an old and valiant soldier, a son of Massachusetts, this circumstance should be handed down to posterity. Those who revere the virtues of the benevolent Howard, must ever remember with veneration the successful exertions of Captain Scott."

He fell at last a sacrifice to a higher spirit than can ever be shewn by mere courage in the field. " In 1793, he went in the suite of General Lincoln, to settle a treaty with the Six Nations of Indians at or near Sandusky — where his health was impaired. In 1796, he was connected with a party in surveying lands on the Black River, near Lake Erie, and in the vicinity of the smaller lakes. They were attacked by the lake fever, and he returned with a division of the sick to Port Stanwix. Finding it difficult to procure any to go back after the sick persons left behind in the wilderness, he determined to go himself, though strongly dissuaded by the physician, who affirmed that he could not return alive. ' I think I shall,' was his reply, ' but if not, my life is no better than theirs.' He succeeded in his benevolent attempt, but died on the 10th day after his return, at Litchfield, N. Y., September 19, 1796, in his 54th year."[*]

This instance, which by no means stands alone in our history, may serve to illustrate the courage which has been always a prominent feature in the character of our citizens. And it has

[*] See N. H. Historical Coll. Vol. I, p. 135.

run through their whole character, distinguishing alike their habits of thought, of social intercourse, of public and private enterprise. In whatever they have undertaken, they have gone forward with the same fearless spirit. If at any time a man has had hard thoughts of his neighbor, he did not whisper it about in private scandal, but the offender was the first to hear it. There has been no secret underhand dealing, but their voices were always loud,* their gait erect, their conduct open. While ready to maintain their own and their neighbor's rights, they have also, it must be acknowledged, never been backward in proclaiming their own merits. Yet they have not been a conceited, boasting race, but men who knew their strength, who judged correctly of their merits, and would not suffer others to destroy or impair their just appreciation.

Closely allied to this was another prominent trait in their character. They were always a high-minded, generous people. Though poor, they were never mean in spirit. Sometimes indeed a foolish pride has been among them. It is related of the wife of the oldest John Morison, that when her husband was building his first habitation in Londonderry, she came to him, and in a manner unusually affectionate, (as is sometimes the custom of wives when they have a great favor to ask,) said, "Aweel, aweel, dear Joan, an it maun be a log-house, do make it a log heegher nor the lave" (than the rest.) A portion of this spirit may have come down to some of her descendants, and perhaps to a few who are not her descendants. But if they have had a little sprinkling of this, they have also been marked by a true loftiness and generosity of soul, which in all their trials has not forsaken them. It mingled with their courage in war. We have seen how prominent it was in the character of Scott.

* Loud talking has always prevailed here; and at least in one case served an important purpose. At Bennington the company belonging to New Ipswich and Peterborough were surprised by an ambuscade of tories, when Lieut. Cunningham of Peterborough cried out with the voice of a lion, " Bring up those four hundred men," which put the tories to flight and left an open passage to the main army.

And in the last war, when our townsman made himself conspicuous in the eyes of the nation by his coolness and gallantry,
in the most perilous enterprise ever ready to " try," and to
succeed where he tried, he gained the confidence of his soldiers and townsmen, by his humane, and generous attention,
even more than by his unquestioned military ability and courage.* The same spirit of liberality guided their intelligence
in politics. When it was proposed in our Legislature to give
some assistance to Dr. Belknap, who was then preparing
his invaluable history of the State, the representative of a
neighboring town objected, saying that he would as soon support an appropriation for the purchase of Tom Thumb. The
next morning your representative,† in the presence of the
House, gave to him a copy of Tom Thumb, adding, that it afforded him much pleasure to be able to make the gentleman a
present so appropriate in size and character to the liberality
which he had shewn the day before. In their influence, great
or small, in high or in low stations, upon the councils of the
state or nation, our people, as a body, have always been on the
side of a liberal, generous policy, whatever might be its effect
upon their private interests. The same may be said of their
conduct as a town. The whole amount of their property at
the present hour would not probably exceed $500.000 ; yet
the amount of taxes this year (and for several years past they

* James Miller, son of James and Catherine Miller, born in 1776, began to
practice law in 1807, and was appointed Major in the U. S. Service in 1808.
The family from which he sprang lived in the Northeast corner of the town;
which seemed cut off from the rest. James Miller, sen., and a twin brother
inherited a farm together, which they lived upon fifteen or sixteen years,
enjoying the produce in common, with no exact division of labor or the fruits
of their labor. The whole family were remarkable for simple hearted truth
and kindness, and at the same time great manliness and courage. Gen.
Miller's history after entering the U. S. Service is too well known to be
given here.

† John Smith, Esq. whose sudden death in 1821 threw a gloom over the
whole town. He perhaps united in himself all the characteristics of our town
in a more remarkable degree than any other man, joining to the gushing
emotions of a child, strong powers of thought, integrity, courage, and an in-
finite fund of wit.

have varied little) is $4.768 22. If to this we add $900 paid for the support of private schools, $1.500 for the support of public worship, and remember that of three hundred and eighty taxable polls only two hundred and six (and many of them by no means the most competent) contribute anything towards the maintenance of religion, we certainly must conclude that our citizens now are by no means backward in their contributions for public objects. In addition to the usual taxes in 1825, $14.000 were raised without great effort for the erection of churches and school-houses, and in roads the town has been liberal almost to excess.

The same spirit has been even more conspicuous in private donations. Losses by fire have sometimes been more than made up to the sufferers by voluntary subscription, and generally he whose house has been burnt has hardly borne a greater share of the loss than many others in proportion to their means. Nor has this liberality been confined to cases of want; but it has often happened that when, by the sudden providence of God, a portion of a man's goods have in this way been destroyed, many whose property was less than what remained to him have cheerfully contributed to make up his loss. There have been, we all know, and still are, mean men among us, but I do not believe that in the history of the town a single instance can be found in which a mean act, public or private, has been for a single day countenanced by the general feeling of the community. It has been my privilege, beyond the lot of most men, to reside among high-minded, generous people, but I have never lived in a place where in thought, speech and conduct, there has been so general a detestation of what is paltry and little as in my native town.

The same spirit has been carried into their quarrels and enmities. Who has ever heard in Peterborough of a sullen, Indian-like hatred, cherished for years or even weeks, watching stealthily for the opportunity of revenge; or of a fawning dislike veiling itself under the semblance of friendship till the secret stab might be given? They have been impetuous in their feelings, and have given way too readily to the impulse of anger ; but the cloud passed quickly off. The storm was too violent to last. They who have quarrelled to-day are to-morrow the more earnest to do each other a kind act. And acts of neighborly kindness in the common intercourse of life have been a leading feature from the earliest settlement of the town. It has made an important part of the good fellowship of the place ; and if the kind office had not its intended effect, instead of going sulkily away and determining to do so no more, they enjoyed it as a good joke, and were quite as ready to repeat the act when a new occasion might require it. A man who had not been long in town, was poor, lazy and shiftless. The neighbors came together and mowed his grass, leaving it for him to do the rest. "It is very light," said the old man, after they went away, " very light, worth mowing indeed, but not worth mowing and raking too," and so he permitted it to lie upon the ground. They were not angry, but simply laugh-ed at his awkward excuse, and for aught that I have heard to the contrary may have mowed and raked his hay too the year following.

This brings me to what has perhaps from the beginning been their *one* trait, standing out from all the rest ; I mean their love of fun. The sun would go down before I could tell half the stories we still have which might illustrate this point.* No occasion, no subject was kept sacred from their wit. The thoughtless and the grave, the old and the young alike enjoyed it. When Capt. Scott had been pierced by five bullets, and his life almost lost, he said the minister had prayed in the morn-ing that their heads might be covered in the hour of battle. " His head," he added, " was safe enough, but the prayer

---

* Moses Morison, the prince of story-tellers, usually manufactured his sto-ries for the occasion. The wit consisted in a wild and comical exaggeration of real facts, and was the offspring of a prolific fancy. It had, however, an unfavorable influence ; for though these stories were told and heard merely as romances, the habit of exaggeration thus produced was likely to extend itself to more serious matters, so that strict verbal accuracy has been too little regarded.

should have extended to the rest of his body.*   Relatives and friends were never spared when they offered a good subject for laughter, but were rather dealt with the more freely.   From the cradle to the grave there was no circumstance which at one time or another did not administer to their mirth.   Even their superstitions had in them a mixture of drollery that took much from their terror.   The bird that was bewitched "only laughed" at the man who shot at it.   They who believed most fully in the reality of the account, and who never doubted that Satan was actually present at the scene, could yet with shouts of laughter, tell, how at a certain place, when Mr. Morison and Mr. M'Lellan, another minister, were there, the evil spirit came, and the bed on which a young woman lay actually rose from the floor, and the ministers, terribly frightened, called upon each other to pray, and Mr. Morison wou d not pray, but at the prayer of Mr. M'Lellan the spirit was driven off.   Our fathers were serious, thoughtful men ; but they lost no occasion which might promise sport.   Weddings, huskings, log-rollings and raisings, what a host of queer stories is connected with them ?-

At weddings† seventy years ago, the groom usually pro-ceeded from his dwelling with his select friends, male and female.   About half way on their progress to the house of the

* A story has been told, which, though perhaps without foundation as a matter of fact, may yet show the extent to which they often indulged their wit in serious matters. The story is, that when they were first forming a church, almost every one propounded was set aside on account of some objec-tion (particularly intemperance), till it became doubtful whether a church could be established, when one of their number rose, and gravely said, " If God chooses to have a church in this place, he must take such as there be."

† The first notice given in town publicly of intended marriage was in 1749. William Ritchie agreed with Alexander Robbe for half a pint of rum, to give notice of his intentions, which he did by nailing the publishment to a beech tree near the old meeting house. The first oral notice (which mode prevail-ed for a long time) was given thus by Alexander Robbe : " Marriage is in-tended between Joan Robbe and Betty Creighton. If ony man or man's man has ony objections, let him speak neu, or forever after haud his clash."

The above, with other curious particulars relating to our early history was furnished me by John Todd, Jr.

bride, they were met by her select male friends. There each party made choice of a champion to run for the bottle to the bride's house. The victor returned to the party with the bottle, gave a toast, drank to the groom's health, passed round the bottle, and the whole party proceeded, being saluted by the firing of muskets from the houses they passed, and answering the salutes with pistols. When they arrived at the bride's house the groom was stationed upon the floor, the father led his daughter, dressed usually in white satin, and delivered her up to the groom, and the rest of the ceremony was performed nearly as at the present time. The evening was filled up with all imaginable sports, and closed with a ceremony which it will hardly do now to mention. This is the way in which our grand-parents were married.

The other merry-meetings then common I cannot stop to describe. Huskings, rollings, apple-pairings, and raisings,* most of those now in middle-life have seen ; and as they think of the new cider, the smoking indian puddings and huge loaves of brown bread, such as our grand-mothers made, with perhaps a whole quarter of mutton, and pork and beans, smoking also from the same oven, and followed by pumpkin, apple and mince, pies, such as they also made, not thin, depressed, or all outside, but thick and plump, and remember the jokes, the plays, the peals of merriment and the sound night's rest that followed, their childhood and the dawning hopes of life rise again ; — the father and the mother, the brother and the sister that are gone come before them, and what would they not give to renew but for once those ancient times ? But they cannot

* At the raising of the third two story house, (in 1764) all the men, women and children of the town were gathered together. After the sills were levelled, prayers were offered, and a psalm sung. Seventeen gallons of rum had been provided, and none of it remained the next morning, except half a pint, which had been stealthily put aside. At a training much later than this, a barrel of rum was placed upon the field, and the head knocked out, so that each, without loss of time, could dip from it what he wanted. Before night an express was sent for more. One man on returning home, said they had had an excellent training, and he believed they were to have more of it the next day, " for he saw many of the soldiers lying upon their arms."

be renewed, and we must soon follow them into the pale and shadowy past, and be known here among our native hills only as a memory more and more dim till it shall vanish clean out.

But I may not dwell on subjects like these. Our ancestors dearly loved fun. There was a grotesque humor, and yet a seriousness, pathos and strangeness about them which in its way has perhaps never been excelled. It was the sternness of the Scotch covenanter softened by a century's residence abroad amid persecution and trial, wedded there to the comic humor and pathos of the Irish, and then grown wild in the woods among these our New-England mountains. I see in them and their genuine descendants the product of the heaths and highlands of Scotland with their border wars, of the rich low fields of Ireland with their mirth and clubs, modified afresh by the hardships of a new settlement and the growing influence of a free country.*

In nothing here was the Irish character more visible than in the use of ardent spirits.† When the entrance of death‡ into the little colony had suspended the sound of the axe, and a strong arm was laid low, all the people gathered together at the house of mourning, and through the long, dark, dismal night watched by the body of their friend. The eldest and most sacred of their number, with the holy volume before him, and with an iron sternness of manner, from time to time administered the words of divine consolation and hope. This was the offspring of Scotland, and betokened at once the sublime and severe character of the highlands. But ever and anon another

---

* See Appendix, No. 1.

† I had thought our ancestors an intemperate people, but it was not so. Some never drank; but there were loose men who would always, when an opportunity offered, get intoxicated, and be quarrelsome. The great body of the people were not in the constant habit of using inebriating drink; but on great occasions, there were few of whom it might not be said, as of Tam O'Shanter, that if they " were na fou," they "just had plenty" — enough to put them in the best possible trim for telling their " queerest stories."

‡ The first death in the town (1751) was of a child, killed by a log passing over him; the second (March, 1753) was of William Stuart, aged 53, who died of fever, and without medical advice, as there was then no physician in the town.

comforter came in, of Irish parentage ; the long countenance became short, the broad Irish humor began to rise, and before the dawn, jokes and laughter had broken in upon the slumbers of the dead. Again at the funeral the same mixed custom prevailed. After the prayer had been offered, and the last look taken, and the coffin closed, spirit was handed round first to the minister and mourners, then to the bearers, and finally to the whole congregation. All followed to the grave. The comforting draught was again administered at their return, and a sumptuous supper prepared. So did they bury their dead in the days of our fathers.

And yet they were a devout, religious people. With their Presbyterian predilections confirmed by the inhuman massacres, extortions and wars through which they had passed, their first object in settling here was that they might be free in their religious faith. And nowhere upon the shores of New-England, every part of which was sought for a religious end, have prayers been offered more fervent and sincere, or the Scriptures read with more constancy and reverence, than in the first rude dwellings of our fathers. The fact, that with such religious teachers they should still have preserved a religious character, shows how deeply those principles had been implanted in their minds. What had clung to them in Ireland, the disposition to humor, rioting and laughter, was only upon the surface, playing there and varying the outlines of the countenance, while the strong granite features of Scotland were fixed deep in the soul. The unbending purpose, the lofty principle, the almost haughty adherence to what they believed true, and high, and sacred, resting on a religious basis, was the real substance of their character. They had foibles, they had weaknesses and errors. But well may it be for us if the refinements of a more advanced society, and a more liberal culture should serve to give grace, beauty and light to the same strong powers of thought, the same courage, though in a different sphere, the same generous elevation of soul, the same vivacity, and above all the same deep, thoughtful religious principle that belonged to them.

I have now before me a list* of four hundred and eighty emigrants, who, scattered through sixteen different states, and if not greatly distinguished, yet holding a respectable place, retain these same strong features. Here, though at times we have felt as if strangers who came among us could only spy out the nakedness of the land after the fruitful gatherings of the harvest, there is still, enriched as the town has been by new accessions, enough to perpetuate the character which we have received from our fathers. Their faults were usually virtues carried too far. The strong mind sometimes became dogmatical, impatient, overbearing; their courage became rashness, their generosity extravagance, their wit levity, their piety was sometimes proud, formal, severe; and all these incongruous excesses were not seldom mingled in the same mind. Such were our fathers, — the substantial elements of their characters well deserving attention, especially in these days of timid virtue; their faults, partly belonging to the times, but more the effect of strong feelings without the advantages of early discipline. At the same time they had in them the rudiments of a real refinement, warm, kind and gentle feelings, — and specimens of politeness were found among them, worthy of the patriarchal age.

A century has gone by since the solitude of our forests was first broken by the sound of their axe; and within that century what events have successively risen upon the world. The old French war, — our own revolution, one of the few great events in the history of man; Washington and his associates, — they have come and gone, and the noise of their actions is like the distant murmurings of the sea, heard inland, when the storm is over, and the waves are sinking to their repose. Then there was the French revolution, filling the world at once with hope and terror, — the rise and fall of that wonderful man, who beginning and ending his life in a narrow island, dethroned monarchs, shook empires, ploughed through kingdoms in his bloody course. During all this while our mountain retreat remained,

* Prepared with much care by Capt. Isaac Edes.

answering only with a faint echo to the tumults that were agitating all the great interests of the world. The common incidents of time passed over it. Our fathers sowed, and with the patience of hope waited the result of their labors, they laughed and mourned, performed or neglected the great work that was before them, and went off one by one to their reward. All of the first, and almost all of the second generation are now gone. The few that linger with us will soon be gathered to their fathers, and no link will be left connecting us with the first settlers of our town. They are going, they are gone; a strongly marked race — bold as the craggy summits of our mountains, generous as our richest fields; impetuous as the torrents that come tumbling down our hills, kind and gentle as the same streams winding through the valleys, and watering the green meadows.

They, and all that they loved, hoped or feared, their intelligence and strength, their warm sympathies and strong hearts, their loud jests and solemn prayers, are gone from their old homes. Their bones repose on yonder bleak hill-side, near the spot where they were wont to assemble, as a single family, to worship the God of their fathers. Blessings rest upon the spot. The old meeting-house, as if it could not longer in its loneliness look down day and night upon the graves of those who had once filled its walls with prayer and song, has gone like them, and the ploughshare has removed every mark of the place where it stood. The grave-yard alone remains. It is overgrown with wild bushes, briers and thistles. There let them in summer spread their shade over the ashes of the dead, and in winter let the winds whistle and howl through them, a fitting emblem of the desolation which must sooner or later strip off every earthly hope. May the blessings of heaven rest still on that spot. Fresher tears may be shed, and more sumptuous ornaments prepared for the new ground, but many are the hearts, of children and brothers and parents which still cling to the old grave-yard, bleak, and wild, and lonely as it is. And some there are, who, when the paleness of death is creeping under their thin gray locks, shall leave the parting charge of the patriarch;

"Bury me with my fathers on the old hill-side. There they buried Abraham and Sarah his wife; there they buried Isaac and Rebecca his wife, there I buried Leah, and there let my bones be laid."

A hundred years have gone by. What unlooked for events in the great wheel of human life shall rise before another century has closed, it were vain for us to inquire. But when a remote generation shall come next to celebrate this day, not one of us, not one of our children, except as a gray and wrinkled relic from the past, shall be found among the living. The Monadnoc then, as now, will catch the first glimmerings of morning, and the last rays of evening will linger upon his bald and rugged brow; the Contoocook will journey onward to the sea; but of all that our hands have wrought, and our hearts have loved, not a vestige will remain as we now behold it. What future good or ill, what storms of civil violence or public war may pass over the land we know not. But so may we live, that the inheritance which we have received, of freedom, truth, intelligence, virtue and faith, may be handed down unspotted to those who shall succeed; and the blessing of Almighty God will go with it, and go also with us.

———————

NOTE.—My object throughout has been to state facts, and not to give opinions. In noticing at the beginning of the discourse, for instance, the long and bitter contests between the native Irish and the Scotch who had settled on their lands, I wished to say nothing of the blame attached to either party. My sole object was to state the facts as viewed at the time by the Scotch emigrants, in order to show the influence upon the character of their descendants. The Irish may have been guilty of cruelty and madness, but it was the cruelty and madness into which a sensitive, generous, enthusiastic people were goaded by oppression.

I cannot let this opportunity pass without expressing my obligations to several members of the Committee of Arrangements at Peterborough, without whose assistance in the collection of facts, this Address, imperfect as it is, could not have been prepared.

NOTES.

No. I.

THE union of opposite qualities, which has sometimes prevented our character from being rightly estimated by strangers, is, with great justice, expressed in the following account of Dr. Jesse Smith, which I have been permitted to extract from a manuscript sermon preached after his death, (Sept. 22, 1833,) by my friend, Rev. Ephraim Peabody, who had been his pastor.

" There were united in him qualities, which, in so eminent a degree, are rarely seen combined. His mind was thoroughly possessed by that foundation of every virtue, — a sense of his own personal responsibility, which governed his life with the omnipotence of habit. Hence that firmness and independence of purpose, which kept its calm and even way, equally incapable of being seduced by the solicitations, or overawed by the fear of man. His iron firmness of resolve seemed almost to partake of obstinacy, till a more intimate acquaintance showed that it was the result of a character, where the mental and moral powers were peculiarly active, but peculiarly well proportioned — where habits of independent, clear thought left no wavering of mind, and the moral energy fully sustained the intellectual decision. And interfused through these more rugged features was a true tenderness of nature, which softened down everything like austerity, and preserved for manhood the simple feelings of the child. It struck men almost strangely, who had seen him only in the struggle of life, to witness how quickly and deeply he was touched by everything that interested others, until it was remembered how much better the firm character preserves the original susceptibilities of the heart, than the feeble. * * * But that which shed beauty over his character and commanded the love and respect of his friends so deeply, was the light and strength it received from religious faith."

In conversation my friend speaks also of his fearless intrepidity of spirit, which, united with the Peterborough humor, that spared no one, and with a frame of mind so vigorous, gave to those who knew him little, the idea of coarseness and levity, hiding at once the nice susceptibilities, deep feelings and lofty principle, which were really, with him, the controlling powers.

8

No. II.

Province of New Hampshire.

To his Excellency, Benning Wentworth, Esq., Commander-in-chief and over his Majesty's Province of New Hampshire; the honorable his Majesty's Council of said Province.

The Humble Petition of us, the subscribers, being Inhabitants of a tract of Land (lying in said Province on the West side of Merrimac River, of the contents of about six miles square, commonly called and known by the name of Peterborough) in behalf of ourselves and others, the inhabitants of said tract of land, most humbly shews — That about the year of our lord 1739, a number of Persons in consequence of a Grant of a tract of land, had and obtained from the Great and General Court or Assembly of the Province of the Massachusetts Bay, by Samuel Haywood and others his associates, granting to them the said tract of land on certain conditions of settlement. And in pursuance whereof a number of People immediately went on to said tract of land and began a settlement, (tho then vary fur from any other inhabitants) which we have continued increasing ever since the year 1739, except some times when we left said Township for fear of being destroyed by the Enemy, who several times drove us from our settlement soon after we began and almost ruined many of us. Yet what little we had in the World lay there, we having no whither else to go returned to our settlement as soon as prudense wood addmitt where we have continued since and have cultivated a rough part of the Wilderness to a fruitful field — the Inhabitants of said tract of land are increased to the number of forty-five or fifty familys, and our situation with respect to terms we at first settled on are such that we cannot hold any Provincial meetings at all, to pass any vote or votes that will be sufficient to oblige any person to do any part towards supporting the Gospel building a Meeting-house and Bridges, Clereing and repairing Roads and all which would not only be beneficial to us settlers to have it in our power to do but a great benefit to people travelling to Connecticut river and there towns settling beyond us—

Therefore we humbly request of your Excellency and Hon' to take the premises under consideration and Incorporate us, that we may be invested with town privileges and immunities as other towns are in this province and your petitioners as in duty bound shall ever pray, &c. Oct. 31, 1759.

> Thomas Morison,
> Jonathan Morison,
> Thomas Cunningham.

Your petitioners beg leave to add, as a matter of considerable importance that the only road from Portsmouth thro this Province to number four is through said township of Peterborough, and which makes it more necessary to repair said Road within said Township, and to make may bridges which they cannot do unless incorporated and enabled to raise taxes, &c.

No. III.

MORTALITY. — The average annual mortality, according to an estimate made from tables furnished by Dr. Follansbee, was, from 1801 to 1806, one in ninety-three; from 1806 to 1816, one in eighty-one; from 1816 to 1826, one in seventy-eight; from 1828 to 1838, one in sixty-eight; which shows a very considerable increase, notwithstanding all the comforts which have been brought in.

EPIDEMICS. — In 1777 the dysentery prevailed severely; in 1800 it prevailed in the north part of the town, particularly among children. Number of deaths, twenty-three. In 1826 it prevailed under a more malignant form among adults as well as children. Number of deaths, fifty-eight.

CASUALTIES. — There have been, since 1751, fifty-eight cases of death by accident; but no person or building has ever been destroyed by lightning.

PAUPERISM. — The first pauper in town was Jane Culberston, 1764; the largest number (seventeen) in 1821. In 1826 the expense was four hundred and ninety-nine dollars and fifty-four cents, and the average annual expense from 1815 to 1836 was about four hundred dollars. Since then the poor have been on a farm purchased by the town, and maintained without cost.

POPULATION in 1775, five hundred and forty-six; in 1790, eight hundred and sixty; in 1800, one thousand three hundred and thirty-three; in 1810, one thousand five hundred and thirty-seven; in 1820, one thousand five hundred; in 1830, one thousand nine hundred and eighty-four; in 1839, two thousand three hundred.

No. IV.

WATER PRIVILEGES. — The following is condensed from Mr. Steele's Report. I regret that an abstract of his full and exact account of the subject is all that our limits will admit.

On the spot where the Peterborough Factory now stands, a Saw and Grist Mill was erected about 1761. The Grist Mill ceased operation in 1817. The Mills were burnt in 1772, and rebuilt.

The South Factory Mills were built in 1758, burnt 1768, rebuilt 1770. Bowers's Mills, — Saw Mill built 1778, Grist Mill added 1781. The Moore Saw Mill built 1780, burnt 1790. Hunt's Mills, — Saw Mill 1799, Grist Mill 1803. Both have ceased. The present Saw and Grist Mill began 1826. The Spring Saw Mill built 1810; James Howe's Saw Mill, 1814; City Grist Mill, 1820; Union Saw Mill, 1823, Grist Mill, 1828; Holmes's Mills, 1827; Upton's Saw Mill, 1837.

COTTON FACTORIES. — The Peterborough Factory, or the Old Factory, or Bell Factory, incorporated December, 1808, started 1810; the brick part with looms added 1817. The first cloth woven 1818, under direction of John H. Steele. It now contains one thousand two hundred and eighty spindles, and forty-two looms, making three-fourth Drilling and Shirtings of No. 16 Yarn, four hundred thousand yards per annum.

The South or Second Factory erected 1809, machinery started 1810 ; now employed in making Satinet Warps and Yarn for the Market.

The North Factory, started 1814, contains now eight hundred and forty-eight spindles and twenty looms, making Drillings and Shirtings of Yarn No. 16, four hundred thousand yards per year.

The Phœnix Factory began in 1813 or 1814 to make Yarn ; looms added in 1822 ; the southern half burned in 1828 ; rebuilt 1829 ; the northern half rebuilt 1831. It contains now three thousand eight hundred and eighty spindles, and seventy-eight looms, and makes Shirtings and Sheetings, part No. 16, part No. 30, five hundred and seventy-five thousand yards per year.

The Union Factory, erected 1823, cost one hundred thousand dollars, contains two thousand five hundred and sixty spindles, and seventy-four looms, and makes seven-eights and four-fourth Shirtings of No. 40, three hundred and fifty thousand yards per year.

The first Clothier's shop was built in 1780 ; the second, 1794 ; the third, 1801 ; the fourth (now Henry F. Coggswell's) 1811 ; the fourth, now run by Thomas Wilson, 1826.

The other Factories which have been or now are in town, carried by water, are the Eagle Factory, Moore & Bement's Machine Shop, the Batting Shop, seven Trip-hammer Shops, an Oil Mill, an Iron Furnace and Stone Shop, a Shoe-peg Factory, two Paper Mills, two Bark Mills, six shops for turning Cabinet and Wheelright work.

The whole Manufacturing power is estimated at three hundred thousand dollars.

PROCEEDINGS

CENTENNIAL CELEBRATION

AT

PETERBOROUGH, N. H.

AT a legal Town-meeting of the inhabitants of Peterborough, holden at the town-house in said Town, October 5th, 1839, the following votes were passed and proceedings had, viz : —

Balloted for and chose JOHN H. STEELE, Moderator, who was sworn to the faithful discharge of the duties of his office by William M. White, first selectman of Peterborough.

On motion, *Voted* unanimously to celebrate, on Thursday, the 24th instant, the *First Centennial Anniversary* of the settlement of the town.

Voted, To choose a Committee of Arrangements, whose duty it shall be to invite such guests as they may see fit, and do and provide all things necessary for the celebration.

Chose Jonathan Smith, David Smiley, John Scott, John Steele, Nathaniel Moore, Hugh Miller, William Wilson, Stephen P. Steele, John H. Steele, Timothy K. Ames, John Todd, Jr., Albert Smith, A. C. Blodgett, George W. Senter, William Follansbee, William Scott, Robert White, Henry F. Coggswell, Alexander Robbe, William M. White, Isaac Edes, William Fields, Frederick Livingston, James Scott, Jonathan Faxon, Reuben Washburn, William E. Treadwell, John Smith.

Voted, To publish in a pamphlet form the Address, together with such other facts and proceedings as the Committee of Arrangements may see fit, and that a copy of the same be distributed to each family in town.

Voted, To appropriate two hundred dollars out of any money in the Treasury, for the purpose of defraying any expenses incident to the celebration ; and that the Selectmen's order on the Treasurer shall be his voucher for the amount so drawn, not exceeding the above named sum.

A true copy from the Records.

Attest, A. C. BLODGETT, *Town Clerk.*

Saturday, October 5, 1839. Meeting of the Committee of Arrangements. Chose John H. Steele, Chairman, and Albert Smith, Secretary.

Voted, That all the sons of Peterborough who have distinguished themselves abroad, be invited to attend the Celebration.

Committee to invite Guests; John H. Steele, Albert Smith, Stephen P. Steele.

Voted, That John Steele, William Scott, A. C. Blodgett, Isaac Edes, John Smith, be added to the former Committee to prepare sentiments for the Celebration.

Voted, That the Secretary be authorised to insert a notice of the celebration in five neighboring newspapers, viz : the two Keene papers, the two Nashua papers, and the Farmer's Cabinet at Amherst.

The following notice was accordingly sent to the above papers.

" The Centennial Celebration of Peterborough will take place on Thursday the 24th instant. An Address will be delivered by the Rev. John H. Morison, of New Bedford, Mass. The exercises will commence at 11 o'clock, A. M. All the absent natives and those who have resided in Peterborough are respectfully invited to attend on this occasion. Peterborough, Oct. 13, 1839."

Voted, That a cold collation be prepared for dinner.

Chose Gen. John Steele, Marshal, with authority to appoint such assistants as he may think proper.

Voted, That a Committee of three be appointed to confer with the Presbyterian Society, in relation to the obtaining of their unfinished church for the dinner.

John Todd, Jr., William Fields, Isaac Edes, *Committee.*

Voted, That a Committee be chosen to prepare seats and make the necessary preparations for the dinner.

James Scott, William Scott, William M. White, *Committee.*

Voted, That a Committee be chosen to contract for and procure the dinner.

Timothy K. Ames, Samuel Swan, William Scott, *Committee.*

Voted, That A. C. Blodgett and James Scott be a Committee to see to the ornamenting of the Meeting-house, and that they invite the ladies to assist, and that they be controlled by their taste.

Voted, That a Committee of three be chosen to invite the Independent Companies, and all the Singers and the Instrumental Music of the town, to take a part in the celebration.

Albert Smith, William Scott, William Follansbee, *Committee.*

Voted, That a President of the day be chosen.

Chose Jonathan Smith, *President;* David Smiley, John Scott, *Vice Presidents;* Albert Smith, *Toast Master.*

Voted, That this meeting be adjourned to Monday, Oct. 14th, at 4 o'clock, P. M.

ALBERT SMITH, *Secretary.*

Monday Oct. 14, 1839.   Met agreeably to adjournment.

Voted, That the procession form at the Town-house on the day of the celebration.

Voted, That the Committee of Invitation be requested to invite all the regular clergymen of the neighboring towns, together with Rev. A. A. Livermore and Rev. Z. S. Barstow, of Keene, and Rev. Mr. Whitman, of Wilton.

Voted, That a Committee of three be chosen to designate the clergymen who shall take part in the religious services of the day.

Rev. Dr. Abbott, Rev. John H. Morison, Rev. J. M. Wilmarth, *Committee.*

Adjourned to Monday, Oct. 21st.

ALBERT SMITH, *Secretary.*

Monday, Oct. 21, 1839.   Met agreeably to adjournment.

Voted, a That Committee be chosen to procure extra seats for the Meeting-house on the day of the celebration.

Chose Frederick Levingston, Jonas Levingston, Riley Goodridge.

Order of the Procession.   The Military: Orator: President and two Vice Presidents: Clergy: Invited Guests: Committee of Arrangements: The elderly Citizens of the Town: Citizens.

Voted, That the above be the order of the procession.

Voted, That all the lower pews of the Unitarian church be appropriated to the Ladies, except those on the broad aisle.

Meeting adjourned.

ALBERT SMITH, *Secretary.*

Thursday, 11 *o'clock, October* 24, 1839.

Sung an *Anthem.*

Invocation, by Rev. Solomon Laws.

Reading the Scriptures, by Rev. J. M. Wilmarth.

Hymn, composed for the occasion by Henry Dunbar, a blind boy.

To thee, O God, we joyful raise
Our songs of gratitude and praise;
Thy mercies like thy dews descend;
O'er all thy care and love extend.

We thank thee, Lord, that thou did'st bless,
Our fathers in a wilderness;
That where the forest darkly frown'd,
The smiling cottage now is found.

We thank thee that to us is given
Freedom, the richest boon of heaven;
And may our country ever be
The land of true equality.

The poor man, in his humble cot,
Is not, O Lord, by thee forgot;
And they whose mansions higher rise,
Receive their blessings from the skies.

Then, Father, grant that we may stand,
Protected ever by thy hand;
And while thy power our life sustains,
We'll sing thy praise in joyful strains.

Prayer, by Rev. William Richie.
Anthem.
Ode, written for the occasion by Nathaniel H. Morison.

Tune— NEW ENGLAND FATHERS — *By Mrs. Hemans.*

Through devious ways, and paths unknown,
Through forests dark and drear,
Our fathers sought these mountain streams,
To plant their offspring here.

They came not forth from princely halls,
To wasting pleasures sold;
They came not as the Spaniard came,
To seek for mines of gold.

But strong in purpose, high in soul,
In virtue armed secure,
They came from homes, affection blessed;
They sought for homes as pure.

Through years of toil, through years of want,
They bravely struggled on;
And lo! the forest melts away;
The sturdy pines are gone.

Their gardens bloom, and fields of corn
In summer breezes wave:
And plenty crowns the smiling boards,
When tempests howl and rave.

But time on hasty pinions flew;
Forgot were toils and woes,
On fair Contoocook's flowery banks,
Their little hamlets rose.

Their names are left for us to bear;
Their spirits, they are fled;
On yonder hill their bones repose
Amidst the slumbering dead.

No monument adorns the spot,
And yet that spot is blessed,
So long as we, their sons, shall own
The spirit they possessed.

Anthem.

Benediction.

Blessing at the dinner table by Rev. Elijah Dunbar; thanks returned by Rev. Peter Holt.

AFTERNOON.

Toast 1st.—The memory of the early settlers of Peterborough.—Let us not forget the perils and hardships which they endured, while we are enjoying, in peace and plenty, the fruits of their labors.

Deacon JONATHAN SMITH (the president of the day,) rose and said:—

" Fellow-Citizens.—The sentiment just read relates to the sufferings and hardships of our fathers, in their first settlement in this place. The orator of the day has related many incidents of the perils they endured, yet the half has not been told I well recollect many of the meetings of the first settlers, at my father's house and elsewhere, when they used to relate the privations, hardships and dangers of their first settlement; and it seemed as though they were enough to break down, their spirits, and cast a gloom over every countenance. Was it so? No. Notwithstanding all they suffered, and all they feared, there was a joyful countenance — there was more mirth, pleasantry, wit and humor, at that time, than at the present. There was another good thing attending those meetings; there was more friendship towards one another; more acts of kindness in relieving each other in their distress. The singing of the old Scotch songs generally closed these meetings.

In truth, their lives were soldier's lives; though they were not so well fed or clothed. These scenes and trials admirably fitted them for brave and hardy soldiers, to fight our battles and gain our independence. If the times and condition of the country raised up men eminently qualified to lead our armies, no less did they raise up soldiers — making them patient of suffering — persevering and confident of success. Had it not been for this, we have no reason to believe that we should have gained our independence. Now shall their sons, well clothed and fed,

9

and at their ease, lose what their fathers so hardly earned?
I hope not; but that the same divine hand that so abundantly
cherished and sustained their fathers in attaining, will also
qualify them to keep and improve the blessings of liberty they
now enjoy; and that another century from this, will find a people *here* improved in all knowledge, virtue and every moral principle, so that our independence will be preserved to the latest
ages.

Music, "Oft in the Stilly Night." Sung by the Choir.

2nd. The Memory of the patriotic Eighty-three of this Town, who signed
a virtual declaration of Independence June 17, 1776.

[A copy of the document alluded to was read by Thomas Steele, Esq., one
of the signers, now in his 86th, year, who gave a short account of every
signer, where they lived, and where they died. No more than three of the
eighty-three remained, namely, Thomas Steele, Esq., Capt. William Robbe
and Benjamin Mitchel, all of them present.]

Music, " Ode on Science." Sung by the Choir.

3d. *The Clergy.* May their united labors, as heretofore, prove a strong
citadel of our free institutions and sacred rights.

Rev. William Richie, rose and said,—

Mr. President.— It is probably expected that I, the eldest of the
clerical sons of Peterborough, should respond to this compli-
ment to the clergy. In the faithful discharge of the duties of
their office, the clergy are necessarily important aids to civil government. Whilst they advance the spiritual interests of men, and
prepare them for a higher and more perfect state of being; they
make them better in all the relations, social and civil, they sustain
on earth. Their ministrations strike at the root of those disor-
ganizing principles and vices which endanger the rights, disturb
the peace, destroy the liberty and happiness of society. The
good done by many other classes of the community is palr ' . :
but frequently the happiest influences of our ministry car .. (
be known until the secrets of all hearts are revealed. 'l . c
will be seen, how often by the faithful ministrations of the cl·'
slumbering conscience has been aroused, incipient crime check ',
languishing virtue revived, and the intellectual and moral natur
awakened into vigorous exercise, and man no longer permitted to
live, a libel on his form and on his Maker.

In the eloquent and interesting Address of this morning, its author, as by enchantment, caused our ancestors, in all their privations and sufferings, excellencies and defects, to pass before us.
The first and second clergymen of this town, we were told, and
some of us recollect, were neither an honor to their profession
nor a blessing to the community. Such examples are however
rare; and their successors still live and fully redeem this order of

men from the reproach cast upon it by their predecessors in this place. Not only the faithful ministrations of the clergy, but their example, is well calculated to guard our free institutions and sacred rights. We are sometimes indeed told the clergy have no concern with politics, and should never leave their proper sphere for one so uncongenial to their sacred office. Party politics, the arts of office-seekers, are sufficiently disgraceful not only to exclude the clergy, but all honest men from them. The man, however, who devotes himself to the ministry, does not by that act surrender his social and civil rights. He has, and should feel, all the interest in the political prosperity of his country, which every good man does; and having no selfish purpose to serve, no office to look for, one would suppose this, added to intellectual acquirements, would render his opinion at least as important and valuable as that of other members of the community. So long as the minister of religion discharges faithfully and independently his duty; expresses fearlessly and courteously all his opinions, without a wish to dictate or control the opinions of others any farther than light and conviction should control them, his influence must be highly beneficial to the religious, social and civil institutions of his country.

I have no wish that former days should return, when respect was paid solely to the office, however unworthy the occupant. Intelligence and character in the clergy should alone command respect and confidence. The clergy have also manifested a deep interest in the cause of education ; and been efficient in elevating the common schools. This is the very corner-stone on which all our valuable free institutions rest. Valuable as are our High Schools and Academies, the Town Schools are the fountains from which knowledge flows to the people. An overwhelming majority of the community and of the electors receive all their education at the town schools. No greater service can be done for the community, than to elevate the standard of education in the public schools. In this important work the clergy have taken an active and leading part. May every class of the community co-operate, until our common schools are what the wants of the community, demand ; affording to every portion of the republic the means of a good education. It is always pleasant to look back to the place where we first acquired a taste for learning. Indeed, every thing which reminds us of the place of our birth, and of those dear parents and friends, whose affection cared for us, when we could not care for ourselves, is deeply interesting. Yes, I have often hailed as a friend the dark Monadnoc, at a great distance, raising his head above the hills and looking far off on the land and on the sea ; and around its barren top have clustered the most delightful associations and reminiscences of by-gone days; of parents and ancestors, whose remains now sleep on the side of yonder hill, on which they uniformly worshipped, and to which they early directed my feet.

1 have already occupied more time than I intended. The rapid advancement of my native town in mechanic arts; the increase of wealth, the improvement in public buildings and private dwellings has given a new aspect to this place. May the cause of education equally advance, giving a permanent glory to the pros' perity of a place we all delight to honor. .1 conclude with this sentiment: —

Intellectual and moral culture,—The only conservative principles of the republic, may they ever have an increasing interest in our hearts.

Music, " *Old Hundred.*" Sung by the Choir.

4th. *Hon. Samuel Smith,*—whose activity, energy, and enterprise, put the first wheels in motion, that have rolled this Village on to its present flourishing condition.

Doct. Albert Smith, rose and said, —

It is with great reluctance and embarrassment that I feel myself obliged to respond to the sentiment just read. I regret to consume any time, in which you might be entertained by others, who are now ready to speak. You have seen fit kindly to notice my father on this occasion — one of the greatest and most important in the history of our town. But the fast creeping infirmities of age have rendered him unable to express, in a manner agreeable to his feelings, the sincere gratification which this kind and flattering notice has given him. You will permit me to speak for him — who, you all know, has heretofore so well and ably spoken for himself.

What he has been and all that he has done, belongs to this town alone : — here he was born and here he has always lived. The sentiment alludes to his efforts as the founder of this village. He did here only what he would have done elsewhere, with such energy of character — such ardor and enthusiasm in his projects; — for he had all the Morison failing of being a great projector, and was withal somewhat visionary. Such men often do great good. It is well that, now and then, an individual can disregard all the minor considerations of prudence and economy and go on fearlessly in his course. Thus great plans are carried out, villages arise, business is increased, and what is ordinarily the work of years, is accomplished at once.

It was thus with my father. Almost any man, with his limited means when he came to this village, instead of building all kinds of Mills, Dams, Walls, Stores, Houses, &c., would, in Scripture language, have counted the cost; and then the progress of this

Village would have been slow, and what was accomplished at one effort, would have been the work of years.

It is now forty-seven years since he first commenced in this part of the village. There was then but one house standing and one family only, near the spot where we are now assembled. All else was in the rude state of nature, untouched and unsubdued. From yonder hill, what a contrast would a view of this place now present! Then all was dreary and desolate. A thick, tangled forest, abounding with lofty pines and hemlocks in all the grandeur of mature age, was flourishing, where now resound the efforts of active and constant industry. There was nothing in the prospect to give pleasure ; for should you look with attention, a high and extensive sand bank, that had withstood the elements for ages, would meet your view ; then you would observe abrupt hills, and the two rivers almost choked with the inroads of the forest. Only now and then might be seen a human being along its narrow and crooked road. The outsettlers of the town could not use too opprobrious terms to express their dislike of the place. But now how changed! from the same spot there would meet your view, (or I am deceived,) one of the most beautiful villages of our country. You would see this beautiful river at your feet, winding its course through highly cultivated fields — at a little distance the green, but, at this time, deeply variegated woods — then the *hills*, the grand hills, some of them rising abruptly, others in a gradual slope from its banks. When your eye rests on the village, you would see the happy homes of hundreds, and of all these, only two, (my parents) remain, who were here in the infancy of the place. Again you would see churches, houses, factories, stores, mechanic shops, and all the busy hum of men — the stir and bustle of business from morn to eve. You would see the evidence of enterprise on every hand, the well marked and not to be mistaken signs of a prosperous and flourishing community. Well might it excite astonishment, that one individual, alone and unaided, and with limited means, should have pitched upon this spot, as forbidding as it then was ; should have reared up such a building of Babel dimensions as justly to be considered the wonder of the day ; should have filled the same with all kinds of mills and machinery then in use and needed by the community; and persevere till he had made a village of his own. But the greater the difficulties, the more ardent and persevering was he in overcoming them. His life has been a lesson of perseverance, whatever other lesson it may have exhibited to mankind. The pecuniary embarrassments which he sustained for years would have prostrated almost any other mind; but he preserved an equanimity through them, that few men possess ; and nothing but the ruthless hand of age and infirmity could depress or break him down. I trust I shall be pardoned for speaking thus. No one *now* can feel any other than sentiments of respect towards him, unless it be of commiseration. For here is a noble mind in ruins. He has now passed the active scenes of life, he has long since ceased to be an object of jealousy or envy to any living being, and soon, in all human probability, must his earthly career be closed. What he has done in life, it is not for me to say. His labors are ended, and whether they be for weal or woe, those who come after him and us will judge.

I offer the following sentiment in behalf and at the request of my father :—

May the present enterprising spirit and increased prosperity of Peterborough — which is so highly honorable and praiseworthy—ever continue.

MUSIC, " *Who is this.*" Sung by the Choir.

5th. *Gen. James Miller.*—A brave man, never to be forgotten by his country, or native town.

Gen. MILLER, rose and said,—

Mr. President and fellow citizens of my native town, — I return to you my sincere thanks for your flattering notice of me on this memorable occasion, an occasion which once more gives me the pleasure of meeting and taking by the hand so many of my old and valuable friends and acquaintances, and of again witnessing the marked improvements of my native place. That her march may still be onward in every useful improvement, is the sincere wish of my heart.

Mr. President, I offer as a sentiment—

May we encourage Literature, revere Religion, and, love one another.

MUSIC, " *Gen. Miller's-March.*" By the Band.

6th. *First Light Infantry and Peterborough Guards,*—A Citizen Soldiery—the best in the World,

Capt. SAMUEL C. OLLIVER, rose and said,—

Mr. President, — My situation is such as to render it inconvenient for me to come forward to speak. But after hearing the sentiment just offered I feel obliged to respond. Although an adopted son of Peterborough, I am proud on all occasions to acknowledge myself one of her sons — even one of her citizen soldiery. Yes, Light Infantry and Peterborough Guards, we have in the sentiment just read the honorable title of a citizen soldiery given us. We are so indeed — members of that institution which gained for us the blessings of liberty and freedom which we now enjoy, and descendants of those noble patriots who won them — with whose praise we are all familiar. We cannot, — we will not, prove ourselves unworthy of the sires who, reared in those valleys, went forth at the first call of their country, met the British lion on the plains of Bennington and Saratoga, and bravely took him. History responds to their heroic deeds; and the echoes of those hills answer nobly to the tune of Yankee Doodle, and fill the air with victory. We are all familiar too with the condition of the American people. Every child knows and adopts the popular sentiment, that ours is the happiest nation on the globe, — and is it not so? We are able to enjoy ourselves independently of others. Although other nations may trouble and even threaten us with destruction, yet we know the strong arm of the militia will defend our families and homes.

It is our own prerogative, and the distinction of the true Yankee, to be prepared to defend, but not to invade. Mark the improvement. One hundred years ago, those limped waters that flow along our river witnessed in their course only the yell of the savage and the howl of wild beasts. Now a civilized and industrious people risé up in clouds before them — a people, too, whose homes and firesides have become academies of useful learning. One hundred years ago, the inhabitants of this fertile soil knew nought but the enslaving maxims that enchain the mind. Now every man is a student. Then none sought to improve by the past, but were content with the pleasures of the moment; — in a word, they were savages. Now all look forward to a nobler and higher state of improvement. Having been sufficiently educated to become instructors of themselves, they reach forward with slow but sure march to jewels that are laid up in store for them. Moreover, we here breathe the pure air of freedom, where all are born equal; where there are no kings, no princes, no nobility, no titles; in a country that is destined to grow on; to fill the Valley of the Mississippi—to spread itself along the Red River, the Arkansaw, the Missouri, climb the Rocky Mountains, descend upon the Columbia, and overspread the shores of the Pacific Ocean with a hundred millions of human beings as free and independent as ourselves. We have something to do in this matter. Mr. President, upon us rests the responsibility for the safe keeping of those institutions and transmitting them untarnished to millions yet unborn.

Fellow Citizens — Citizen soldiers: — When our country with all her noble institutions, shall cry Defend — Are we Ready? Aye, Ready.

Mr. President—Permit me to offer the following sentiment—

The Fair.—It is but fair, that the Fair partake of our fare on the present occasion.

Music, " *Gen. Washington's March.*" By the Band.

7th. *Our Absent Sons*, — We gladden at your prosperity, we mourn if you attempt to do evil,—though we grow old we do not forget you.

Exeter Oct. 22, 1839.

Gentlemen, — I regret that it is not in my power to accept your invitation to attend your Centennial Celebration on Thursday. Nothing, I assure you, could give me more pleasure. I am sure none of the sons of old Peterborough would enter more into the joyous feelings of the day. I have known her nearly as long as any of her children still alive, and yield to none in attachment. I have experienced nothing but kindness and confidence from her ever since I was capable of knowing good from evil; and I pray Heaven to reward her for all her goodness to me. Allow me to offer this sentiment :—

Peterborough, — May she be as distinguished in the next century for moral worth, as she has been for intellectual superiority and business enterprise in this.

I am, gentlemen, with much regard, your obedient servant,
JEREMIAH SMITH.

New York, Oct. 17, 1839.

Gentlemen,— I assure you, with the most perfect truth and sincerity, that I received the invitation with heart-felt satisfaction, considering the place whence this gratifying testimony proceeds. It being the place of my early and late associations, it demands the expression of my profound and grateful acknowledgments. It occasions me painful regret not to be able to accept the invitation, and I cannot conclude without tendering to you and those whom you represent, my respectful thanks for the honor done me on this occasion. Permit me, Gentlemen, to propose the following sentiment —

Peterborough, — What was she a century ago — what was she half a century ago — and what is she now? May her industry, enterprise, improvements, prosperity and happiness continue to advance onward for centuries yet to come.

Your Obedient Servant,
DANIEL ABBOTT.

Boston, Oct. 17, 1839.

Dear Sirs, — Accept my hearty thanks for your invitation to the Centennial Celebration at Peterborough. I should most certainly attend, were I not denied that pleasure, by ill health. But, gentlemen, I shall not be unmindful of so interesting an event; for I intend to celebrate the day at my own residence in Boston. I shall be *with you* then, though not actually in my native town.

Your kind letter brought to my mind many pleasing reminiscences of days gone by — of the scenes, the times, the associates and friends of my youth. The Wilsons, Steeles, Mitchells, and Smiths, — the Morisons, Stuarts and Moores — the Millers, Whites, and many other worthy citizens, whose names are familiar to you, appeared before me. They had a rugged path to walk; but they were industrious and persevering. They were open-hearted, public spirited and independent men; and it is gratifying for me, a native, though non-resident of Peterborough, to know, that the present inhabitants are the true representatives of such predecessors.

On the 24th inst., and while you are publicly rejoicing, I shall fill my glass with wine in honor of the day, in remembrance of the first settlers, and my old comrades and friends, and to the health of their descendants, and the present inhabitants of the town; giving this sentiment:

The Pioneers of Peterborough, — Let us cherish their memories, and teach our children to emulate the labors and virtues of the first settlers of the town.

Renewing to you, Gentlemen of the Committee, and through you, to the citizens, my regret that "though with you, I shall not be *there*," on the occasion in question, I remain an ardent friend of my native town, and

Most respectfully your obedient servant,

SAMUEL GRAGG.

———

BELFAST, OCT. 15, 1839.

Gentlemen, — A short absence prevented the receipt of your letter a day or two. But the first occasion is embraced to say, that the pleasure of attending your Centennial Celebration would overcome all objections as to distance, if it were not that the Court of Common Pleas sits in this County on the first Tuesday of next month, and that will prevent attendance.

With leave, the following sentiment is offered.

The Town of Peterborough, — May her prosperity be as rapid and lasting as her streams.

Yours, with sentiments of high respect,

JOHN WILSON.

———

CINCINNATI, OCT. 18, 1839.

Gentlemen — I am much obliged by your kind invitation to be

10

present at the Centennial Celebration at Peterborough. It would give me a peculiar pleasure to be there on an occasion so interesting, and especially as I should find myself among many old friends, but it will be wholly impracticable. If there were time, (I received the letter yesterday) I could not come. Our lecture term is at hand, and I must be on the ground.

Be pleased to present my affectionate regards to the Rev. Mr. Morison, if he be the same gentleman who was once my patient; and my sincere respects to my old friends, the recollection of whose kindness years and years agone, I fondly cherish.

Very respectfully, your friend,
R. D. MUZZEY.

———

BOSTON, OCT. 16, 1839.

Gentlemen, — Your kind letter of the 7th instant, inviting me to join the citizens of Peterborough in the celebration of the approaching Centennial Anniversary of the town, on Thursday the 24th inst., was received in due course of mail. I feel highly gratified with being remembered on this occasion by the inhabitants of my *native* town; the town where I spent the pleasant hours of my early childhood; where the remains of my beloved parents, now long since mingled with its dust, were deposited. But I should feel a much higher gratification, if my daily engagements would permit me to meet with my brethren, the sons of the town, and interchange with them the feelings which belong to such a relation, and respond, in such manner as I might be able, at the moment, to sentiments suitable to such an occasion. Since this gratification is denied me, I take pleasure in saying, that I feel proud in numbering myself, here in Boston, among those who hail from the "Granite State," the birth-place of a Statesman, who has acquired for himself the exalted appellation of "The Defender of the Constitution;" and more especially among the sons of the town of Peterborough, the nativity of many industrious, frugal, enterprising agriculturalists, the "*bone and sinews* of our country," and other men, who have eminently excelled in the manufacturing art, at the bar, and upon the bench, in the senate and on the field. That the town of Peterborough may flourish in the coming century, as she has during the past, and continue to send forth her sons with the spirits of their fathers to excel in all the useful occupations of life, is the sincere sentiment of one of her sons, and gentlemen, your brother,

I. P. OSGOOD.

———

FRANKLIN, OCT. 21, 1839.

Gentlemen, — When I received your kind invitation to attend the Celebration, I was determined to do so; but circumstances

75

have occurred since, which render it impossible for me to attend.

Although I cannot be present on the occasion, my heart and soul will be with you. I claim to be a native son of Peterborough, and feel proud of my maternal home. The occasion brings to my mind many pleasing recollections of bygone days, the days of my childhood, when seated with others of my father's family around the winter evening fire, listening to the traditionary tales of the first settlement of the town.

I will conclude this communication by proposing the following sentiment.

The adopted sons of Peterborough. — However distinguished or exalted may have been many of her native sons, may her adopted sons be equally distinguished.

Yours, in the bonds of affectionate brotherhood,

JOHN ANNAN.

———

NEWPORT, OCT. 22, 1839.

Gentlemen, — It would have given me great satisfaction to meet my early associates, and join with them in the festivities of that occasion.

Peterborough is dear to me, and I feel proud of being recorded among her sons, of whom so many have distinguished themselves in the different professions and departments of active life. She has within my own short recollections sent forth four or five respectable Clergymen, and fifteen or sixteen Lawyers, four members of Congress, and four or five respectable Physicians. She can point to the Hon. Jeremiah Smith, for a long time Chief Justice of the Superior Court of Judicature, truly a sage of the law, and a former Governor of this State, as one of her sons; and to Doctor Muzzey, now of Cincinnati, as not less distinguished in the medical department; and to Gen. Jas. Miller, not less distinguished in our military annals.

Suffer me, in conclusion, to offer the following sentiment:—

The citizens of Peterborough,— May they continue to cherish literature, and the arts and sciences — may they be distinguished for their morals, and those virtues which elevate and ennoble man; and may she send forth men who shall protect and defend the rights of our country, and perpetuate our free and liberal institutions.

With sentiments of respect and high consideration,

Yours truly,

AMASA EDES.

BATH, OCT. 19, 1839.

Gentlemen,— I received your invitation a few days since to attend the Centennial Anniversary Celebration of the settlement of the town of Peterborough, on the 24th inst.

My attachments to my native place are strong, and though I have spent a large portion of my life elsewhere, those attachments have not diminished, nor has a link of the chain that bound me there ever been severed.

It would give me great pleasure to be present with you and participate in the Celebration, but it is otherwise ordered; and though I may never again see the place of my birth, or again mingle with my fellow-citizens there, for whom I have such strong sympathies and attachments, I may be present with you *in spirit* on this occasion.

I was early taught to entertain high respect for that hardy and enterprising band, who in 1739 and the ten following years, established the settlement of our native town. They possessed certain traits of character of high excellence, (doubtless mingled with faults of as strong a character,) yet those of excellence so far predominated as to give a marked and distinctive character of excellence to the people of the town.

I trust some one of her many talented sons will be found ready, on this occasion, to do justice to their memory and character. Permit me, gentlemen, to offer you the following sentiment :—

May the generation that now is, exhibit all the excellencies of character, without any of the faults, of the generation that is past, for the instruction of those who are to come ; that the town may continue to have a name and a praise, for the worth of her citizens, when those present are gone from the stage and rest with their fathers.

I am, gentlemen, very truly yours,
JONATHAN SMITH.

———

NEW YORK, OCT. 19, 1839.

Gentlemen,— Your kind invitation of the 8th instant came duly to hand. I have delayed replying, hoping to do it in person; but I very much regret my engagements are such as I cannot remove, and will consequently prevent my attendance.

That you will have a gratifying Celebration I have no doubt, and that you may, is the sincere wish of
Yours, very truly,
JEREMIAH SMITH.

———

BOSTON, OCT. 22, 1839.

Gentlemen,— I have delayed giving you an answer, in hopes of being able to be present on the interesting occasion, and now I am truly sorry to find myself unable to leave my business affairs at this time ; otherwise it would afford me the greatest pleasure to be present.

It is pleasant to visit the home of our childhood at any and all times, but especially on such an occasion as the present.

Your ob't servant.

DAVID CARTER.

BALTIMORE, OCT. 15, 1839.

Gentlemen,—Nothing could give me greater pleasure, than to be present at your celebration, but circumstances will necessarily prevent. Allow me therefore, to express myself, though now adopted elsewhere, still a son of my native town, good and true to the core in feeling, and every wish for her prosperity, and to propose the following sentiment, as my *representative* among you :—

Our native town, — Her *intelligence,* the *boast;* her *success,* the *joy ;* her *hills,* memory's dearest *shrine ;* her *all,* the *pride* of her absent sons.

With great respect, I am your's, &c.

HORACE MORISON

BALTIMORE, OCT. 15, 1839.

Gentlemen,—Your letter of the 9th instant was received, inviting me to attend a Centennial Celebration in Peterborough on Thursday the 24th of Oct. Nothing could give me more pleasure than meeting on that occasion my townsmen, the inhabitants of Peterborough, and her many distinguished sons from abroad; but circumstances beyond my control render it impossible. I trust, however, I shall be there in spirit, and, like a true-hearted son, enjoy in imagination the festivities in which I can take no part. I hope my native town will accept in my absence, the following lyric * from one of the humblest of her bards, as a fit offering on such an occasion.

Accept for yourselves personally my warmest regards, and believe me truly your fellow townsman.

NATHANIEL H. MORISON.

MUSIC, " *The Winding Way,*"—Sung by Messrs. Carter and Dunbar.

8th. *Non-resident owners in our Manufacturing establishments,* — For their liberality in aiding the public and private institutions of Peterborough, we return them our sincere thanks.

BOSTON, OCT. 22, 1839.

Gentlemen, — I have received your letter of the 16th inst., with a polite invitation to attend the celebration of the First

----

* Inserted on p. 64.

Centennial Anniversary of the town of Peterborough, on the 24th inst. I much regret that it will not be in my power to attend said celebration, as it would afford me much pleasure to meet my friends and acquaintances at that place.

I have known Peterborough for about sixty years, and observed with pleasure its rapid growth in population, agriculture, manufactures, arts, sciences, literature, &c. &c.

My first visit to Peterborough I will relate, merely to show some of the changes that have taken place since my recollection. Fifty-nine years ago last April, a man with a drove of cattle passed my father's house in New Ipswich, on his way to a pasture for his cattle in the town of Hancock. Being in want of assistance to drive his cattle, and seeing a flaxen haired boy at the door, he bargained with my father that I should assist him on his way as far as the mills in Peterborough, distance ten miles ; for this service to be performed by me, my father received *ninepence, lawful money ;* we arrived at the mills — a rickety saw and grist mill, standing on the site where the Peterborough Factory now stands, about four o'clock. The man of cattle then offered me half as much as he had paid my father, and a night's lodging, if I would go on with him through the woods three miles to Taylor's Tavern. I readily consented, and pocketed the cash. At that time there was only one house (Doctor Young's) between the mills and the tavern. All the rest of the way was a dreary wilderness. But enough of my first visit to Peterborough.—I propose, with your permission, Gentlemen, the following toast : —

The first Settlers of the town of Peterborough, — The Smiths, the Wilsons, the Steeles, the Morisons, and many others ; celebrated for their industry, perseverance, prudence and honesty. Also their sons and grand-sons whether at home or abroad ; they have done honor to themselves, to their native town, and to their country. Their virtues and talents have shed a lustre on every profession, political, judicial, ecclesiastical, medical, military and scientific.*

I have the honor to be, most respectfully, gentlemen, your obedient, humble servant.

SAMUEL APPLETON.

P. S. Gentlemen, if you have not on hand more toasts than time, I beg leave to propose the following : —

The first Matrons of Peterborough, — Who, like the matrons of King Solomon's time, laid their hands to the spindle and distaff, made fine linen and sold it to the merchants,† and looked well to the ways of their household.

* Among my acquaintances may be reckoned Judge Smith, General Wilson, Doct. Smith of Cincinnati, Rev. Mr. Morison, General Miller, &c. &c.

† Fifty years ago the writer of this kept a small store at New Ipswich, and exchanged tea, sugar, coffee, pins, needles, &c., for home spun fine linen, made by the matrons and fair daughters of Peterborough.

Also, their fair daughters, of the third and fourth generation, who without handling the distaff, by the almost magical use of the spinning jenny and the shuttle, can clothe themselves in silks and fare sumptuously every day.

BOSTON, OCT. 19, 1839.

Gentlemen, — Your favor of the 16th inst. came duly to my hands, and I accept and thank you for the invitation to attend the Centennial Anniversary of your Town on Thursday next.

I fear that it may be impracticable for me to be absent from Boston at that time, and shall much regret if such shall prove to be the fact. In any event, my sympathies and feelings will be with you ; for I have witnessed with lively interest the growth and improvement of Peterborough, and find it my pride and pleasure to associate with her sons.   Very respectfully, yours,

SAMUEL MAY.

Should I be prevented being with you, on the interesting occasion, allow me to offer through you as a sentiment : —

The Town of Peterborough, — Forward in the ranks of Agriculture and Manufactures ; high in the scale of education, morals and religion ; she has sent forth her full quota of eminent and excellent laborers in Church and in State. May she go on " prospering and to prosper."

BOSTON, OCT. 23, 1839.

Gentlemen, — This will be handed you by my son. I regret very much that I cannot be with you to-morrow, but having only within a few minutes returned from a journey of some fifteen or sixteen days, it is impossible that I can have that pleasure. I have many pleasant reminiscences connected with Peterborough. Born, as it were, upon the borders of the town, her brooks and rivers were familiar to me, for I was in the habit of fishing from them the wily trout, before factories were hardly thought of, other than the then common ones for manufacturing meal and boards. I should there find myself surrounded by many old friends and acquaintances, and might perhaps point out in the assembly, the man who used to purchase of me the skins of the muskrat,* which I entrapped to supply myself with change, for election and training days — and I trust I should then meet my much respected and ever valued friend † — Peterborough's most enterprising son — who, when I became of age, and was about to leave New England, to seek my fortune and business in western wilds, unsolicited, took me by the hand and established me in business with himself in Keene ; a change which no doubt has

* Jonas Loring ; for a long time the only hatter in town.
† Samuel Smith, Esq.

much promoted my prosperity and happiness, and for which I trust I shall ever feel grateful.

With manufacturing in Peterborough I can claim an early connexion, as well as one of more recent date. More than forty years ago I was an *operative*, and used *to set card teeth by hand*, for one of her citizens, for which I was paid fourpence a pair, *not in cash*, but " store pay." By close application in my leisure hours, I could set about one and a half or two pairs in a week. I was an owner in the Peterborough Factory, and was present at the commencement of its operations in 1810, and that I believe was the Second Cotton Factory in the State; since then I have been interested in *most* of the factories established there, and have done business to a considerable extent, for them *all*.

In many towns, where manufactories have been established within the last twenty years, the inhabitants have looked upon them, and especially upon the proprietors who were non-residents, with jealousy and distrust; but it has not been so with the citizens of Peterborough. They have been governed by more enlightened and liberal views, and with few, very few exceptions, they have fostered and aided the corporations by all the means in their power; and from them the proprietors abroad have ever received the most kind and courteous consideration and support, for which they are entitled to, and through you I would most respectfully present to them, my sincere acknowledgments. To you, Gentlemen, personally, for your kind invitation to be present on this interesting occasion of the Centennial Celebration, I tender my thanks, and offer the annexed sentiment to be used as you may deem proper.

Very respectfully, your obedient servant,
ISAAC PARKER.

Peterborough.—Prosperity to her people, to her manufactories, her *fur trade* and her *fisheries*.

MUSIC, " *Hill of Zion.*" Sung by the Choir.

9th. *Our adopted Citizens.* — May we never in action or in word say to any one of them, — thou art the son of a stranger.

JOHN H. STEELE, Esq., rose and said, —

Mr. President, — Had I the ability to do justice to my own feelings, or to the feelings of many others who like myself are adopted citizens of Peterborough, the present occasion would have been eagerly sought. No minor considerations could have prevented me from embracing this opportunity, to return thanks in the warmest language of the heart, for the many proofs we have received, not only of your kindness and open handed hospitality, but for the free, warm-hearted welcome invariably extended to every stranger whose fortune it is to make his residence among you.

No diversity of opinions has at any time prevented that cordial interchange of sentiment or free discussion, which is the parent of every improvement. All here meet as men should meet. No fancied distinctions or differences of opinions, are suffered to destroy that sociability, which is at once the pride and boast of Peterborough.

The stranger, as well as native, share alike the honors and pleasures of society. No wonder then that your sons, where-e're they roam, in whatsoever situation they may be placed, whether on the tented field, in the senate, on the bench, in the pulpit, at the bar, following the plough, or hammering on the anvil,—all cheerfully own their native home, all proudly hail from Peterborough.

Mr. President, — if the sentiment which has brought me forward, is to be considered as a call *now* made on the native citizens of this town, never, in action or in word, to say to any one of their adopted citizens, " thou art the son of a stranger," it will not convey a reproach either now, or in times gone by. No, Sir, nearly thirty years' residence among you enables me to say, that for the past you can have no reflections to cast ; — the stranger is here sure to find a resting-place, a *Home.*

To those who have never wandered far from their paternal firesides, I would say ; you know not the feelings of the immigrant, the longing desires of the homeless stranger. No one who has wandered far from the home of his youth, but must have felt a loneliness, a depression of spirits, a yearning after his native land, an almost irresistible impulse to return to the place that gave him birth, — it is of little consequence where that place may be, — whether on the borders of the burning desert, amid the chilling blasts of the frozen North, or the yet more fatal stagnant swamps of the South. Let him be a forced or willing exile ; let him have received the kindest, or the most cruel treatment that the ingenuity of man can inflict ; all, all, cannot, will not, and let me add, should not, wean him from his native land. He that can forget the land that gave him birth, must be unworthy to be called an adopted citizen of any other. Such a man deserves not the sympathy of others. On such a being the kind and generous greetings of his adopted home is lost. He careth not whether you say to him thou art welcome, stranger, or, that " thou art the son of a stranger." Far different are the feelings of him who never hears the name of his native land without emotion. Although alive to the interests of the home of his childhood, he will not neglect or forget the interests of his adopted home. By such a man a cheerful, hearty welcome will be duly appreciated ; it will cheer him on, and bring forth whatever there may be of

11

the man in him; while a different reception, if it did not destroy, would paralyze his future efforts, and perhaps extinguish forever all the energy of his character. His usefulness would be impaired, his previous acquirements lost, and all his future prospects blasted; the home of his adoption would only be able to number one more human being among them, who would probably live a life of wretchedness instead of one of usefulness, and die a neglected, forgotten stranger.

Yes, fellow-citizens, on you in a great measure depends the usefulness of every stranger who may permanently settle among you. It is true you cannot give youth to the aged, neither can you make the stupid active, nor yet entirely wean the sluggard from his slothful ways; but you have, time and again, by your open-heartedness, not only encouraged all who were disposed to help themselves, but have effectually rebuked, both by precept and example, the vicious and evil inclined. Many a youth, who from previous associations had acquired a thoughtless, if not a ruinous habit of extravagance, has been by the example of your industry reclaimed, and made to bless the day that led him to choose this as his abiding place.

Mr. President, — The allusions of the orator of the day to the Old Meeting-house on yonder hill, brought forward in bold relief the remembrance of one of Peterborough's brightest, noblest sons; one whose influence has contributed much towards giving a distinct character to the town. A friend, whose departed spirit, if permitted to leave the realms of bliss, where it long since has taken its abode, is now within these walls. The noble, manly, generous spirit that animated him while here, must now look down on this crowded assembly, while with a tear on his manly cheek, ready to drop, and wash away all that his purer soul finds to condemn, his cheerful eye eagerly scans this animated collection of human beings, and returns thanks to the author of all good for the prosperity of his native town.

Mr. President, — I hardly need add that I allude to your departed brother, John Smith, Esq. If Peterborough can boast of a better, more useful, brighter, purer hearted son than was John Smith, I know him not. That she can point to many whose exterior, both in dress and address, comes much nearer to what is generally termed a finished gentleman, no one will doubt. But where now is the man, who never lets a human being pass him unheeded; whose ever active mind, and ready talent, can draw forth alike the budding powers of childhood, or those of ripened age; who is ever ready to aid, council, or direct, with wisdom, purse, or hand, his fellow man? Such a man was John Smith. With an address which to a stranger appeared as rough and rugged as the mountains which surround his native town, he possessed a heart as tender and pure as ever animated the breast of man. To him

I owe more than I can express. He was not only a friend, but a father. He taught me to believe that there is nothing impossible; nothing that a willing mind, and active hand, cannot accomplish. I yet seem to hear his voice reproving me for saying, *I cannot do it!* He would say " Steele, Steele, you booby, why don't you try, and not stand there looking as if you were in a trance ?" Shade of my departed friend, permit me to say that your reproofs, councils, and aid, have not, I hope, been entirely lost.

But, Mr. President, I detain you, and keep back others, who are much abler, from giving to you and this assembled multitude matter more pleasing and better suited to the present occasion. Yet I must beg your patience for a few minutes longer. I cannot sit down, Sir, without saying one word to the Ladies. In attempting so to do, I am not compelled, but willingly throw myself on their well known generous kindness. — It has so often been said, that it is believed at least by every gay Lothario, that the way to win the good will of the Ladies is to flatter them. Is this so, Ladies? If it is, I had better stop where I am. Should I at this time of life attempt to turn flatterer, it would, it must prove a failure. No, I shall not attempt it. My fate has been cast in a sterner mold ; nor do I believe one word of this slander. Such a libel on your good sound sense and well known discriminating powers, must have been penned or uttered by one of those nondescript beings, frequently seen hovering around the fair daughters of the land, like a gay, gaudy butterfly around the beautiful half blown rose, and like that transient insect is chased away by the approach of the first active useful busy bee. Would you know them, mark well their confident air, their tight bound waist and gay clothing, the closely cramped toes, the never forgotten silk or embroidered kid gloves, the rattan or other useless switch. Useless, did I say? Not so, its repeated raps on their well polished boots or full cushioned legs, will at least give you warning that a flatterer is approaching ; and if age has furnished him with a beard, you will be almost sure to see the face half covered with a carefully curled pair of whiskers. Although they are called, as I suppose, by way of derision, " Ladies' men," avoid them as you would a viper. They are mere peacocks. Their hats may be of the latest fashion, but there is nothing in their heads. With the lighter, vainer portion of young and thoughtless females, who, like themselves, think gay clothing must make their charms irresistible, they may pass for men. To such, if any such there are among the many bright faces around us, I have nothing to say. They must be left to smoother tongues than mine.

It is to the more staid and useful I would say, go on as you have done ; encourage your husbands, sons and brothers, in every thing that is manly and generous.

To you are or will be committed the destinies of our town.

The results of the past are before us ; the changes and improvements are great. Will the coming century produce as great ? No one here can answer. No one here will in all probability live to see. One hundred years hence, when your descendants assemble, as we this day assemble, to commemorate the Second Centennial Anniversary of their native or adopted town, will they be able, as I believe you *now* are, to say that all the good our mothers taught us, we have kept and practised. To your Mothers, as well as to yourselves, do we mainly if not entirely owe that public spirit, that love of order, that open, generous, manly bearing, which always did, and still does, distinguish your husbands, sons and brothers.

To your influence are we, the adopted citizens of Peterborough, indebted for our privileges. Your influence enables us to say that this is truly the home of the stranger.

Guard well the rising generation. To you, to your guidance, it must be committed. *Must ?* No! I take back that word, and say, to none other should so important a trust be committed. Without your fostering care, without the anxious care and instruction of a mother, what would man be ? Deprive man of his natural and best companion, *Woman*, he would then be, or soon become, a fit companion for the tiger. Degrade and debase woman from her proper sphere, and man at once sinks to the level of a savage. Give her full and free scope, and man rises to a higher destiny as fast or faster than generations pass away.

Mr. President, permit me to offer as a sentiment,—

Peterborough,—May she ever continue to be, as she has heretofore been, the Stranger's Home.

Rev. Elijah Dunbar, rose and said,—

Mr. President, — An adopted son of Peterborough, following the example of our respected friend who has just spoken, would also briefly respond to the kind notice which has been offered. My adoption, which was confirmed forty years ago, yesterday, *you* well remember. The venerable Council of the ordaining Clergy, with a very few exceptions, are gathered to their fathers; and it is with a great, though a mournful satisfaction, that we welcome the *last surviver*, in this immediate vicinity, the Rev. Mr. Ainsworth, to our Celebration. It reminds us of his venerable colleagues, whom we shall see no more, till we meet on the shores of eternity.

My long residence here, my long continued and intimate connection with generations past and present ; the continued kindness and support I have experienced; and the identity of national descent, from Scotch origin, almost persuade me that I am a native.

The enterprise, the benevolence, and the liberality of the natives of Peterborough form a distinguished and highly honorable characteristic.

Among the evidences this day exhibited, permit to notice the handsome *military display*. It may remind us of those who fell and those who triumphed in the war of 1755; of the enterprise, perseverance and intrepidity of our Revolutionary heroes; and of the more recent *glory* of the battle-field of Bridgewater.

I would offer this sentiment :—

The Citizen Soldiery of Peterborough. — May they continue to cultivate the *martial* spirit — may they be ever *prompt*, at their country's call; and he that hath no sword, let him sell his coat and buy one.

M_r. THOMAS PAYSON, rose and said,—

Mr. President, — The *toast*, to which my valued friend, an adopted son of Peterborough, has so *justly* and *happily*, although, considering the time is so far spent, rather too *lengthily* responded, I had intended to have noticed in a more extended manner, than, from the lateness of day, is now in my power. That friend has handsomely anticipated something, which I contemplated to say, on this occasion, as *one* of the *fortunate*, though *lately adopted* citizens of this *memorable* town.

I will, however, with your good leave, state, in a few plain words, what my impressions of the inhabitants were, before I knew them.

In early life it was my chance to make acquaintance with one of the natives of Peterborough, and to have no very favorable report of some others. He possessed not a few of the *reputed* characteristics of his fellow-townsmen, which the distinguished orator of the day has so justly and impartially portrayed.

This *personal* knowledge of *one* and *historical* reputation of others, predisposed me to entertain no very favorable opinion of the place and people. Nor was this opinion lessened by the story of the outrageous application of *Lynch-law* to an unhappy clerical subject, who had by that same people for many years been retained in the sacred office, to his own and his people's disgrace.

With these things fresh in my recollection, it so happened that a few years since I was called on to consider the proposal of making this same Peterborough my place of *rustication*.

Can any one of this respectable auditory who hears me, indulge in *wonder*, that, under such circumstances, I should feel a strong repugnance at making my future residence and closing my life among a people so famous? I assure you, Sir, that repugnance was great, and that this was among the last places in New England, of which I had any knowledge, that I should *voluntarily* have made my home.

Circumstances, however, overruled my volition and repugnance. Twelve years since I removed to this town. How great were my surprise and disappointment, after a short residence here, in the appearance of the place, and in the character of the people, I hardly need now repeat. I had looked at them through a foggy medium. I had judged of the *whole* by a *part* only. Instead of being stared at as a *stranger*, and treated as the *son* of a *stranger*, I found myself among a friendly set of men, was taken cordially by the hand, *kindly*, and even *respectfully* received, and treated as a *native son* or *brother ;* the people, with as few exceptions as can be found in any other place, open hearted hospitable, independent and intelligent ; and more than usually *well read* — with good feelings and good manners. Modern degeneracy had not yet reached them. Had I come earlier in life among them, and had possessed a reasonable talent for improvement, I might have profited more by their society and example. As it is, I owe them much. May the legitimate fruits of such social qualities constantly crown their future honest enterprise and labor.

In conclusion, allow me to offer the following toast :—

The Pioneers of Peterborough in the 18*th century, their Posterity of the present day, and the Generation yet to come* — May their progressive advancement in knowledge, morals, the arts of life, and religion, prove commensurate with their years and their privileges.

Music, " Home! Sweet Home." By the Band.

10th. *The Agriculturists, Mechanics, and Merchants of Peterborough,* The three great founts of our industry and prosperity.—May they ever encourage and support each other.

William Scott, Esq., rose and said, —

Mr. President, — I will make a few remarks in answer to that part of the sentiment just given, touching the class of citizens to which I am proud to belong, and to which belonged those bold Pioneers, the first settlers and fathers of the town. The cultivation of the earth is the primitive and the most honorable employment in which men can engage. Every individual should feel an interest in agriculture. Considered as an art, it is the foundation of all others. The wealth and unparalleled prosperity of this country may be attributed to the industry of the tiller of the soil. From this source all real wealth is derived. The employment is healthful and invigorating to body and mind, and operates powerfully and beneficially upon the morals and constitutions of those engaged in it, giving a right and permanent tone to our national character. I believe that open hearted generosity and hospitality are more generally found to animate the rough, home-spun farmer, than the more polite citizens of cities and villages ; and if they take temperance and virtue for their guide, the tillers of the soil enjoy more of ease, more of the real luxuries of life, and undisturbed sleep, than the debilitated inmates of comp-ting-houses and city work-shops. They may justly be said to be the happiest class of people on earth. The torch of liberty has ever burned with a purer light on the hills and mountains, among the farmers, than in cities and villages. This was the case in Switzerland in the days of William Tell, and thus it was in this country in the struggle for independence. The agriculturalists compose, in a great measure, the present defence of the Union. Standing upon the soil, which they own and cultivate, they are ever ready to catch their muskets, and march to defend the liber-ties of the country. They can be relied upon with more cer-tainty, in case of sudden invasion, than those engaged in com-merce and trade, not being so likely to suffer loss by sudden fluc-tuations ; for from these sources the farmer derives only a part of his luxuries, the necessaries of life being produced by the labor of his own hands. Notwithstanding these high claims in favor of the pursuit of agriculture, it has been considered in years gone by, as a low, unpopular, if not vulgar, employment. This undoubt-edly arose from the sudden accession of wealth amassed by merchants and commercial men, and the high price paid for labor in and about our manufacturing establishments. These causes led many of our young men to forsake the occupation of their fathers in hopes of finding a more speedy road to wealth, prefer-ring the meanest drudgery in the shop or compting-house, to the hoe and rake. To such an extent has this unbounded desire of wealth been carried, that our compting-houses in particular, have become full to overflowing. The slightest revulsion in trade turns loose upon society numbers of no profession, no occupa-tion ; being so long habituated to a city or village life, to return to the occupation of their fathers, they become dead weights upon the community, mere idle loafers, a name unknown in the days of our fathers.

But, Mr. President, I believe the days in which agricultural pursuits have been considered degrading, are numbered. Many of our most respectable mechanics, as well as professional men, have, within a few years, turned their attention to the tilling of the soil, occupying the hours that they can spare from the calls of their customers or books, in the healthful as well as profitable pursuit of agriculture. This has caused a rise of lands, particu-larly in the vicinity of this village, almost beyond belief. This course, continued throughout the country, will create a taste for agriculture, and will prove instrumental in causing more of our youth to embark in this laudable pursuit. The time is not far distant, I hope, when our schools and colleges will be more anx-ious to instruct our youth in agriculture, than in the dead and al-most useless languages.

A few words to my brother farmers, and I will close. While

88

we are pursuing that best and most independent of all arts, agriculture, let us not forget the duties which we owe to our fellow citizens. Let us aid with a liberal hand and cheerful heart, the various useful institutions of our country; encourage and support our mechanics and merchants. As to the lawyers and doctors, may we be so fortunate as to need but little of their assistance.

I conclude by offering as a sentiment :—

The Laboring portion of our Citizens.—May their numbers be increased by accessions from the ranks of those of no profession, until all become usefully employed.

Mr. A. C. BLODGETT, rose and said,—

Mr. President, — after so distinguished a display of talent and eloquence as that which has preceded me, I must acknowledge I feel somewhat diffident in attempting to make any response to the sentiment which has just been offered. But, sir, we have some thoughts which we won't conceal, some feelings which we can't disguise. Perhaps, sir, no one feels more than I do how much we owe to each other, not only in regard to our welfare and prosperity in business, but in the kindnesses and courtesies of civil and social life. It is but a few years since, when I was as it were but a youth and just entering the drama of the world, that I left my native home and came a stranger among you; "but a welcome smile and a friendly face" seemed to whisper in fancy's ear that, though a stranger, I should not long be among strangers. You have been pleased to take me by the hand and adopt me as a citizen, and now I feel that I am one among my townsmen, who have come together within this temple, this day, to commemorate that epoch in our history which lies buried beneath the dust and darkness of a by-gone century. One hundred years have now rolled away since our forefathers first broke the gloom of that wilderness, which for thousands of years before had hung brooding over the land upon which we now live, move, breathe and tread; and, standing as we now do on the line which divides one century from another, looking backward through the vista of years, let us for a moment contemplate Peterborough as she then was, a howling and hostile wilderness. The same old Contoocook, whose waters now whirl by us, passing on through flowery vales and banks of green, moving and aiding in her course almost every mechanical invention and enterprise — was then overshadowed by sylvan bowers and her shores trod by the feet of savages. In the midst of this wild and romantic scene the echo of the white man's axe is heard by day, and his lowly hut receives his wearied frame by night; but he receives not there the feast to which as a reward for his daily labor he is entitled. "His needy couch and frugal fare," are all the luxuries of his home and fireside. Day after day the echo answers back again, until here and there is to be seen a little cleared spot, a log house and a field of grain springing up in the wilderness. They have now, to be sure, a home in the forest; but they have not the comforts nor conveniences of civilized life. Afar off in the world lay those blessings in *store*. For more than thirty years did they seek abroad, in other towns, all their merchandise.

Their numbers at length invited hither the merchant; and how willing and ready the farmers and mechanics were to sustain him, you, Mr. President and fellow citizens, can judge for yourselves by the specimen of calico which the orator has exhibited to you this day, and for which one hundred pounds of butter was paid. And for the same compensation at this day I would cheerfully part with twenty such dress patterns of the same quality. But, Sir, I do not wish to be understood by this that farmers and mechanics are not as ready and willing to sustain the merchants as they were at that day. I say it to you, sir, and to all this assembled multitude, in the language of sincerity and truth, that I have ever found them ready to pay a fair and honorable consideration for all necessary articles of merchandise. It is not they, nor the want of encouragement and support from them, which retards the prosperity of the merchant; but it is the spirit of jealousy, envy, rivalry and competition which exists among the merchants themselves, that is so detrimental to their prosperity. If the merchants here do not prosper as well and heap up golden treasures as fast as they wish, let them blame and censure each other, and not the farmers and mechanics who have patronized them with a generous hand and liberal heart. But, while I as a merchant feel grateful for the liberal patronage so generously bestowed upon me, I cannot think the reciprocity is all, or should be all, on one side. If I buy one hundred pounds of butter or cheese, or bushels of corn or grain of the farmer, and pay him a fair market price, and he buys a corresponding amount of goods of me, and pays a fair price, I am at a loss to know whose business it is, or should be, to say, "thank ye." I owe to him, and feel under the same obligations, which man should ever feel due and bound to perform towards his fellow-man, that of philanthropy and good will. The great object of us all is to be free, independent, and happy; but there is a mutual dependence which we have upon each other, and a mutual advantage arising from it, which has a tendency to refine and perfect those blessings, not only as relative to business, but in all the relations of life. Trade in this place has had its ups and downs, its lights and shades Its whole history is checkered o'er with the smiles and frowns of fortune; for here fortunes have been lost and won. Stores have multiplied from one to seven; the amount of goods has increased from two thousand to thirty thousand dollars. Circumstances have invited merchants from abroad, and fortune wafted them away to crowded cities and climes that echo farther west. Here people have commenced trade in early life and continued until it was in the "sear and yellow leaf," and their children have risen up and become merchants abroad in the world, and ere another century shall roll away, who can dream of the changes which time may bring about? All of us, who are now on the stage, will have passed through the dark wilds of life. Our stores, with all of our existence that is mortal, will alike have crumbled into dust beneath the ravages of time. As the old Persian monarch, when he sat upon the brow of the mountain " which looks o'er seaborn Salamis " and surveyed the vast multitude of human beings which composed his army, wept, that ere a hundred years should pass away, not one among them all would be numbered among the living ; even so might we at this time and on this occasion weep, that of all who are here assembled, not one will come forth a living monument at the next Centennial Jubilee to rehearse to posterity the scenes of this day. It will be for their children and their children's children, who may rise up in generations to come, to read from history and tell from tradition.

My worthy friend who has preceded, (Mr. Esq. Scott,) has portrayed to you in glowing colors, "in thoughts that breathe and words that burn," the merits of his own profession, and how much the community and country are indebted to them for their strength and prosperity. They give a complexion to the age, they are the stamina of the land, the palladium of civil liberty and the bulwark of public safety. Now, Mr. President, I acknowledge the truth and force of the gentleman's remarks. Every year that rolls round, furnishes us with satisfactory proofs, as we behold the fruits of their industry and enterprise, springing forth in flowers of beauty ; and like that virtue which lives when beauty dies, ripening into the fruits of promise, while their sons and daughters are rising up to call the nation blest, But may I not, sir, with equal justice and pride, claim the same honors and merits not only for my own profession, but also for the mechanics, who, though silent and voiceless on this occasion, are by the works of their hands daily showing forth to the world, in characters of living light, too bold and indelible to escape observation and admiration, how much this town and the whole country are indebted to them, for their present flourishing and prosperous conditions. Under their auspices and emulation, as a community and nation, we are constantly rising in the scales of laudable improvements, and marching on from strength to strength in the fulness of prosperity. " All are but parts of one stupendous whole," a mutual co-operation and combination of men. Business and professions have their benign and salutary influence in heightening the charms of society, imparting a zest to life, and a weal to the land. Fortune, and the fate of things, has allotted to us different parts to perform, on this transitory stage of action; and all are alike honorable in themselves and essential pillars and props to each other. The professors alone elevate or depress the professions. Every noble feeling should then animate us to " act well our parts ;" so that in all the various callings of genius and fortune, we may look back upon the past without remorse, and forward to the future without fear ; setting an example to the generations who may succeed us, which they shall be emulous to imitate, by making some laudable pursuit the object of each passing moment, with constant endeavors to grow wiser and better to the end of time. I will trespass no longer, Mr. President, upon the patience of the audience. I will only, in conclusion, offer as a sentiment : —

Mental Endowment. — May its bright and chastening influence be breathed into all ranks of society, and equalize all business and professions.

Music, " *Mehul.*" Sung by the Choir.

11th. *The Music, Vocal and Instrumental.* — May their combined and animating influence never be exerted for any but a useful purpose.

Music, " *Multitude of Angels.*" Sung by the Choir, led by Mr. Milton Carter.

12th. *Woman.* — The last and best gift of God. May her amiable qualities teach men to love virtue.

Gen. John Steele, (Marshal of the day,) rose and said, —

Mr. President, — We look back to the wives, sisters and daughters of the early settlers of this town. No hardship could discourage, no allurements divert them from industry. Although all their industry could not procure them costly attire, it gave them and their families comfortable clothing, and assisted their husbands and brothers to convert the wilderness into a field for the growth of rye, potatoes and flax, and aided in the raising of sheep and cows to help in the support of the family. The mother taught her children that strength, honesty and virtue, were the rubies that were highly to be valued; that virtue and industry were the smoothest path to journey through life. They took much pride in keeping their children trim and neat, and regularly sent them to meeting. If they had shoes, it was well ; if not they must go that part of the season which was comfortable, without. No excuse about dress, even if the feet were bare, would satisfy. If the youngster said no, the little bunch of rods was pointed to, and the youth thought it best not to have them taken down. After meeting, inquiry was made of the children, about the text and sermon. And they were seated to say the *catechism.* Let us look back to the time when the eighty-three husbands and sons signed the virtual declaration of Independence, (which was read this day by one of the signers.) Cut off from all connection with the parent country, they were deprived of every article, not only of luxury, but of clothing. They had to depend entirely on the large or foot wheel, with their skill in turning them. Not one word of complaint was heard. When a neighbor or friend came in, the buzzing wheel was set aside, and a cheerful conversation introduced. Soon came the song, (very often the Battle of Boyne,) and many others, as each one had a store of them. They passed the evening in cheerfulness. If a stranger was among them, they made great exertions to treat him with the best they had. They sometimes talked on religion; were not very superstitious, although some few thought that a good sound Presbyterian stood the best chance in a future state. One of the elderly * mothers on hearing that the Reverend found fault with young men and women for dancing together, said, "the minister had better take his dram out of his own bottle, play his own fiddle, and let the young people's innocent amusements alone."

When the old ladies saw their childrens' children walking in the path they so highly recommended, it brought a smile of approbation on their wrinkled countenances.

Ladies of the present day! will you go back and view those old fashioned women, though poorly dressed? I trust you can find something to venerate, something to admire in their characters. When you consider the vast importance of your precepts, and example to your families and society at large, will you not think with those good old dames that honesty, wisdom and virtue, are the most precious ornaments to grace the youth of the present day?

MUSIC, "*The Mellow Horn.*" Sung by two Young Ladies.

13th. *Emigrants.* — Well may we be proud of them. They exhibit in manhood, characters that began their infancy on these our sterile hills. May they never forget the land that gave them birth.

Gen. JAMES WILSON, rose and said, —

Mr. President, — I regret that I am called on to respond to the sentiment which has just been announced, and received with so much approbation by this great assembly. On looking over the list of sentiments yesterday, I was informed that the one just read was designed to call out that highly respected, time-honored gentleman, the Hon. Jeremiah Smith of Exeter; a man who feels proud of the place of his nativity, and who on all proper occasions has a good word to say of, and for, old Peterborough. We should have been delighted to have seen that venerable and venerated man here, and to have heard from him, in his usual

* Mrs. Gordon.

eloquent and forcible manner, his reminiscences of by-gone times. He has indeed grown old, but not old enough yet to forget any good thing. His mind is richly stored with varied learning, and his knowledge of the early history of the town, the peculiarities of its early inhabitants, his great fund of wit and anecdote connected with the first settlers, very far exceeds that of any living man ; and there is now no one of the emigrants who could so well give an apt response to your highly complimentary sentiment as that worthy octogenarian. I was heart-pained to learn, last evening, that his attendance is prevented by physical infirmity. In his absence I could have wished that another highly respected son of Peterborough, of the Smith family, had been here to have spoken in our behalf. I allude to one more nearly allied to you, Mr. President, — your eldest son, my most esteemed friend. We are of nearly the same age. Our friendship dates back to the days of our childhood. Our intimacy commenced in that little square hiped-roof School-house, that formerly stood between your homestead and the homestead of my honored father. It was an intimacy, in the outset, characterized by the ardor of youth, and grew with our increasing years into the strong and unwavering friendship of mature manhood. There has never been a moment's estrangement. For thirty years no frost has chilled it, nor can it grow cold until the clods shall rumble upon our coffins. Glad indeed should I have been to have met, once more, my friend here, to have grasped him by the hand, to have looked upon his slender form and his pale features, to have listened to the tones of his clear voice, to have caught and treasured up the sentiments of a mind as clear as the atmosphere upon the summits of our native hills, and a heart as pure as the fountains that gush from their base. From the sad tidings that I hear, of his declining health, I fear that I shall never meet him on this side the grave. May a merciful God bless him.

Well may Peterborough express her joy at the success of her absent sons, and pride herself upon them, when she numbers such men as these among them.

Your sentiment, Sir, breathes the prayer that we, the emigrants, may not forget the place of our nativity. I can hardly realize that I am an emigrant. True, Sir, a wave of providence has taken me up, wafted me onward, and cast me upon land not far distant. Although my domicil is in another place, it is here that I seem most at home. It is here that I enjoy all those pleasures derived from early recollections and early associations. It is here, that every natural object that meets my eye, has some story to relate of high interest to my mind ; — here every house, and tree, and stump, and stone, hill and brook, presents to me the image of some old, familiar, well loved friend. It is here that I meet my earliest friends, and their greeting seems warmer and more cordial here than elsewhere. It was here that I first enjoyed that substantial Peterborough hospitality, so well under- stood and so highly appreciated by every one at all acquainted with the people of the town some thirty years ago. Let me not be understood, Mr. President, as drawing a comparison unfavor- able to the good people with whom I am in more immediate in- tercourse at the present time. No Sir; I reside among an ex- cellent and a worthy community, to whom I am bound in a large debt of gratitude. They have manifested towards me a kindness and a confidence vastly beyond my merits; and I am sure they will not esteem me the less for finding me susceptible of emotion at the recollections and fond associations of my childhood.

Forget Peterborough! How can I forget her? Why, Sir, I was born just over *there*. The bones of my ancestors, both pater- nal and maternal, are deposited just over *there*. And among them *there*, repose the remains of *my Mother*. Oh! Sir, it would be cold and heartless ingratitude, to forget the place where one's earliest and best friend slumbers in death: —

> " Ingratitude ! Thou marble-hearted fiend,
> " More hideous, when thou show'st thee in a child,
> " Than the sea-monster! "

Spare me, Oh! spare me such a reproach.

My prayer to Heaven is, that when this eye shall grow dim, this tongue become dumb; when these lungs shall cease to heave, and this heart to throw off a pulsation, then this head and these limbs may be laid to crumble down to dust by the side of thine, *my Mother!*

Sir, when I learned some few weeks ago, that it was proposed to celebrate this Centennial Anniversary of the settlement of my native town, I resolved to be present; and in the expectation that I might be called on for a word, I began to search the by-places and corners of my mind to ascertain whether any thing connected with Peterborough history had been stored away there, that might be brought out to contribute to the interest of the occasion. When I heard who was appointed to address us, I had my fears that all the choicest and gayest flowers would be forestalled. My worst fears have been more than realized; but I have learnt one thing with sufficient certainty, — that it is hopeless to attempt to keep any good thought out of the reach of the Morisons. They have a wonderful tact at seizing every grand, intellectual concep- tion, and surprising facility in appropriating it exclusively to their own use. If, in my effort to brush up my recollection, I have had the good fortune to find any thing worthy of remark, I find myself anticipated by my learned friend, the orator, to whose elo- quent and excellent Address we have listened with so much inter- est. I ought, perhaps, to rejoice that the evening is so far ad- vanced, that I have time only for a very few words, since all that

I could have said has been so much better said by that worthy gentleman.

We have heard of the patriotism of our ancestors, of their unanimity in sustaining, and devotion to, the American cause in her early efforts for free government. They sought for a government of equal and impartial laws. Permit me to relate to you an anecdote illustrating their profound respect for sound laws.

My Grandfather, as you know, Mr. President, kept a tavern in a small house, the shape of which sets all description at defiance; but its rickety remains are still to be seen upon the farm of your townsman, Capt. Wm. Wilson. A number of persons being assembled at his public house, an occurrence happened, not unusual in the town at that time, to wit, a fight. There was a blow, and blood drawn. The defeated party threatened an immediate prosecution, but the spectators interposed their friendly advice, and a reference of the matter was agreed to by the parties. Five good men and true were designated as referees, who undertook to arbitrate upon the momentous matter. A solemn hearing was gone into. Every person present was inquired of as to the fact. After a deliberate hearing of the parties, their several proofs and allegations, the referees awarded that the aggressor should pay the cost of reference by a full treat for all the company, and give as damages to the injured man, for the blood lost, an equal quantity of cherry rum, which they appraised at half a pint. Ill-blood is sometimes created between the parties to a lawsuit, that continues to circulate in the veins of succeeding generations. No such result followed the Peterborough lawsuit above reported. The wisdom of the referees was universally commended, as manifested in their liberal award of damages, and their sagacity highly extolled for the discovery of an adequate and proper remedy for healing the wound inflicted upon " the peace and dignity of the State." The referees, the parties and their witnesses all separated perfect friends.

We have heard that one of the prominent traits of the early inhabitants was a fondness for fun. It was on all occasions sought after, and it mattered little at whose expense it was procured. The name of one has already been mentioned, famous for his singular cast of mind and his witty sarcasms — " Old Mosey Morison." I at this moment have in mind an anecdote, which, by leave, I will relate, and if I omit the name of the individual upon whom the wit was perpetrated, I suppose the *chief marshal* of the day will take no exception to the relation of the story. Mosey Morison was here universally called, in common parlance, " Uncle Mosey." A young gentleman of no small pretensions to learning and high standing in this town, some forty years ago, went to the town of Nelson, then called Packersfield, to instruct a winter school. In the course of the winter " Uncle Mosey " happened to call at the store of a **Mr. Melville**, where a large number of the people of Packersfield were assembled, and there met the young Peterborough school-master. The school-master accosted him in the familiar salutation of " How do you do, Uncle Mosey." The old gentleman, looking away, and manifesting no sign of recognition, replied in a cold, disdainful tone, " *Uncle Mosey! Uncle! to be sure! I'm na Uncle of yours ; I claim na relationship with you, young man.*" On his return to Peterborough, Mr. Morison related the incident to his blood relations, the Smiths, who asked him why he denied the relationship of the school-master. " *Why,*" replied the old man, " *I did na wish the people of Packersfield to understand that a' the relations of the Morisons were consummate fools.*"

I fear, Mr. President, that I am taking too much time in the relation of Peterborough stories. I will detain you with only one more. At one of the stores in town, upon a cold winter's night, quite a number of the people being present, the *toddy* circulated freely, and the company became somewhat boisterous, and, as usual, some of them talked a good deal of nonsense. An old Mr. Morison,* who plumed himself, (and not without much reason,) upon his talking talent, had made several unsuccessful attempts to get the floor, (in parliamentary phrase,) and the ear of the house. The toddy had done its work too effectually for him, and he gave it up as desperate, and taking a seat in a retired part of the room, he exclaimed in utter despair, " *A' weel, a' weel, here ye are, gab, gab, gab, gab,— and common sense maun set ahind the door.*"

I have watched, with intense interest, the wonderful improvements that have been carried forward in my native town within the last thirty years. When I was a boy, a weekly mail, carried upon horseback by a very honest old man by the name of Gibbs, afforded all the mail facilities which the business of the town required. Now, Sir, we see a stage coach pass and repass through this beautiful village every day, loaded with passengers, and transporting a heavy mail. Your highways and bridges have been astonishingly improved, showing a praiseworthy liberality on the part of the town to that important subject. Your progress in agriculture, manufactures, and the mechanic arts, exhibit striking evidence of the progress of improvement. Look abroad now upon the finely cultivated fields, the substantial fences, the comfortable, yea, elegant dwellings, the superb manufacturing buildings, the splendid churches and seminaries of learning ; and in view of all these let the mind for a moment contrast it with the prospect which presented itself to the eye of the first settler as he

---

* Jonathan, the first mechanic in town, and the first male child born in Londonderry.

attained the summit of the east mountain, one hundred years ago. Then not a human habitation for the eye to repose on over the whole extent of this basin-like township, — one unbroken forest throughout the eye's most extensive range. No sound of music or hum of cheerful industry saluted his ear. It was only the howl of the savage beast, or the yell of the still more savage man, that broke the appalling stillness of the forest. What a wonderful change hath a hundred years wrought here, and what unshrinking energy of character was requisite to induce the commencement of the undertaking!

Some of the old objects of interest to me in my younger days are gone; their places indeed have been supplied by more expensive and elegant structures. Still I must say I regret their loss. And let me ask, Mr. President, are you quite sure that the loss may not manifest itself in some future time? I allude, Sir, to the loss of the old church on the hill *there*, and the old beach tree that stood hard by. I look, even at this period of life, upon that spot with a kind of superstitious reverence. Many are the noble resolutions that young minds have formed under the shade of the old beach tree. Intellectual indolence is the prevailing fault of our times. Under the old beach, in my young days, the great and the talented men of this town used to assemble, and there discuss with distinguished power and ability the most important topics. Religion, politics, literature, agriculture, and various other important subjects were there discussed. Well, distinctly well do I remember those debates carried on by the Smiths, the Morisons, the Steeles, the Holmeses, the Robbes, the Scotts, the Todds, the Millers, and perhaps I may be excused here for adding, the Wilsons and others. No absurd proposition or ridiculous idea escaped exposure for a single moment. A debater there had to draw himself up close, be nice in his logic and correct in his language to command respectful attention. Abler discussion was never listened to any where. Strong thought and brilliant conceptions broke forth in clear and select language. They were reading men, thinking men, forcible talking men, and sensible men. Bright intellectual sparks were constantly emanating from those great native minds; and falling upon younger minds kindled up their slumbering energies to subsequent noble exertion. The immediate effect of those discussions could be easily traced in the beaming eye and the agitated muscles of the excited listeners. It was obvious to an acute observer that there was a powerful effort going on, in many a young mind among the hearers, to seize, retain and examine some of the grand ideas that had been started by the talkers. This rousing of the young mind to manly exertion, and aiding it in arriving at a consciousness of its own mighty powers, was of great advantage where the seeds of true genius had been planted by the hand of nature. If any of the

13

Peterborough boys, within the last thirty years, have attained to any thing like intellectual greatness, my life on it, they date the commencement of their progress from the scenes under the old beach tree. A thousand times have I thought, Mr. President, if I had the world's wealth at my command, 1 would cheerfully have bartered it all for the ability to talk as well as those men talked. Antiquity may boast of her schools of philosophy. The present may point to her debating clubs and lyceums, and talk loud as it will of modern improvement ; — give me the sound good sense that rolled unrestrained from eloquent lips under the old beach, and it is of more worth than them all. I shall always respect the spot where it grew, and even now it grieves me to see the green-sward, that sheltered its roots, torn too' roughly by the ploughshare.

I had purposed, Mr. President, to have asked the attention of the audience to some few remarks upon the all-important subject of education. Old Peterborough has hitherto given her full share of educated men to the public, and I cannot but hope that she will not now permit her neighbors to go ahead of her in this particular. The shades of evening, however, admonish me that I must not trespass further. I must tender my thanks to the audience for the very kind and polite attention they have given me during the remarks I have felt constrained to make at this late hour in the afternoon. Allow me to say, in conclusion : —

The sons and daughters of Peterborough, native and adopted, — In all good deeds may they prove themselves worthy of the noble stock that has gone before them.

At the close of Gen. Wilson's speech, when it was so dark that the audience could hardly distinguish each other's faces, a general invitation was given to attend a ball in the eveining at Col. French's. On motion of Albert Smith, the meeting was adjourned for a hundred years. And with shouting and the clapping of hands — joy mingling with many pensive thoughts — the assembly of fourteen or fifteen hundred persons separated to lie down in their graves long before the next meeting shall be held.

Monday, Nov. 4th. 1839.

Met greeable to notice.

Voted, That the proceedings of the Celebration, — the Sentiments and the Responses, be published with the Address.

Voted, That the Committee of Invitation, viz : John H. Steele, Albert Smith and Stephen P. Steele, be requested to write to those absent who responded to sentiments, and also obtain and prepare for publication all the remarks made by others.

Voted, That a copy of the Address be deposited in each of the following places for safe keeping, viz : In the Library of Dartmouth College. In the Library of Harvard College. In the Collections of the Historical Society of New Hampshire, and with the Antiquarian Society at Worcester, Mass.

Voted, That this meeting be dissolved.

ALBERT SMITH, *Secretary.*

The Committee return their thanks to the citizens of Peterborough, for the confidence reposed in them, and hope that the services rendered will prove acceptable.

To the fault finders, if any such there be, we would say (in the language of one of the Boys who assisted in clearing away the decorations of the Church,) " You are welcome to this, but at your next Centennial Celebration you may do it yourselves.

CPSIA information can be obtained
at www.ICGtesting.com
Printed in the USA
BVHW04*1210180918
527831BV00013B/901/P